Praise

"Most of us don't like ~~being used~~ especially if we're used by others, or even the enemy of our soul, for negative purposes. But we fulfill our created purpose when we fully open ourselves to being used by God for His work and glory. Dan Nehrbass shows the difference and gives insights for being used the right way—by the Lord."

—Jim Daly
President of Focus on the Family

"When I was fourteen years old, I cried out, 'God, I know You are real and I want You to use me for Your purposes, but please don't make me a pastor or a missionary!' Now fifteen years into full-time vocational ministry, I am thankful that God agreed to use me but didn't listen to my caveat! In Daniel Nehrbass' *Who's Using You?*, we gain valuable insight into how to be used by God as a vessel for His great purposes. Nerhbass' book reminds us that we are either being used by God, others or the enemy. With only a short life to live, I want every moment to count and be used by God. This book encourages me on this journey."

—Matt Doan
Reach Pastor of Calvary Church
Santa Ana, CA

"Daniel Nehrbass not only gives us a fresh and powerful framework for viewing our lives, faith and daily patterns. He also helps us see the small, often unnoticed choices that become the watershed between a life that is ultimately useless and one that is well-used for things of eternal value."

—Jedd Medefind
President of Christian Alliance for Orphans
Author of *Upended: How Following Jesus Remakes Your Words and World*

"*Who's Using You?* allows you to explore the infinite imagination God has in using our lives for His glory, others' blessings and our fulfillment. With exciting stories and biblical principles, you can begin to dream how your life can be used and others' lives can be changed. I can't wait to get this book into the hands of our congregation."

—Dr. Bill Staffieri
Senior Pastor of Beachpoint Church
Adjunct Professor, Biola University

"Dostoevsky once wrote, 'people are people and not the keys of a piano.' Dan Nehrbass understands this truth, but also understands that humans have a telos, an end for which we were created. Just as a hammer was made to pound nails, so we were created for God's glory. Nehrbass helps us understand the beautiful music God desires to create in our life. Take, read and be challenged."

—Dr. Hank Voss
National Director of Church Planting
The Urban Ministry Institute

WHO'S USING YOU?

Dear Daria,

I know you have found the pleasure of being used by God – enjoy.

Dan

WHO'S USING YOU?

Making Yourself Available for God's Use

Daniel Nehrbass

CLC PUBLICATIONS
Fort Washington, PA 19034

Who's Using You?
Published by CLC Publications

U.S.A.
P.O. Box 1449, Fort Washington, PA 19034

UNITED KINGDOM
CLC International (UK)
51 The Dean, Alresford, Hampshire, SO24 9BJ

ISBN (paperback): 978-1-61958-203-3
ISBN (e-book): 978-1-61958-204-0

Unless otherwise noted, Scripture quotations are from the Holy Bible, New International Version (NIV®), © 1973,1978, 1984 by International Bible Society. Used by permission of Zondervan Bible Publishers. All rights reserved.

Unless otherwise noted, Scripture quotations are from the Holy Bible, English Standard Version® (ESV®), © 2001 by Crossway Bibles, a publishing ministry of Good News Publishers. All rights reserved.

Unless otherwise noted, Scripture quotations are from the Holy Bible, New American Standard Bible® (NASB®), © 1960, 1962, 1963, 1968, 1971, 1972, 1973, 1975, 1977, 1995 by The Lockman Foundation. All rights reserved.

Italics in Scripture quotations are the emphasis of the author.

Dedication

For my wife Kristina, whom God has used
as His primary instrument in shaping me.

Contents

Part Three

Used by the Enemy

Part Four

Used by God

Part Five
How to Be Used by God

Acknowledgements

I am grateful for my father, who inspired me to write and taught me how to do it. I am indebted to Chuck Schussman for being an excellent proofreader and sounding board for my ideas. You force me to do better work. Thanks also to my brother Kenneth Nehrbass for your skill as a writer and proof-reader. This book would not be possible without the excellent training I have received from Ron Hammer and David Augsburger.

Many thanks to the wonderful friends with whom we have been privileged to work at Oak Chapel in Marion, Indiana, at Sea Ridge Church in Irvine, California and at the First United Methodist Church in Fountain Valley, California. You have exemplified what it means to be used by God. Though the names have been changed, all the personal stories in this book are true. Thanks to those who allowed their stories to be told here.

Introduction

I Was Used

My wife and I are fortunate to have experienced "a day that changed everything."

I met Kristina in our eighth-grade math class. We dated throughout high school and college, and after a seven-year courtship, we were married at the age of twenty. Most people get married when the relationship is in a "honeymoon phase." But because we had known each other for so long by the time we got married, we had already experienced much of the disillusionment often associated with the first few years of marriage. Still, the early years were near miserable. In retrospect, we can see that we began our marriage at our lowest point. During the second year, we had a recurring pattern on Saturday nights where we would begin arguing at midnight and continue until three in the morning. We argued about how to use our time, how to keep the home, how to spend money—and especially about how the other person should have acted or spoken. This did not well equip me to preach at church a few hours later on Sunday mornings. The pattern continued for a few months, and somehow the supernatural significance of the timing escaped me.

At the time, I imagined that the arguments were the result of two individuals with independent thoughts and agendas who had difficulty communicating or agreeing with each other. When couples come to me for marriage counseling, this is nearly always the way they envision their arguments as well.

But then the creativity with which I was able to hurt my wife startled me. I became aware that I had what seemed like a supernatural ability to say the perfect words to hurt her in ways deeper than anyone else could. Words came out of my mouth that exceeded my own creativity and intelligence in their power to manipulate and sting. I used words that so successfully caused pain, they could only have been cooked up and hand-delivered to me on a platter from hell.

I do not say this to excuse myself from blame, only to acknowledge that my wife and I were not the only parties interested in the events that took place on those Saturday nights in our solitary house in rural Indiana.

Up until this time, I had imagined that my wife and I were sitting in two chairs, both opposite each other, and these were the only chairs in the room. But when I recognized the depth of hellish wording, call it "hurtful creativity," that had entered our house on those nights, I realized that the image of two chairs had to be adjusted. A better picture would be that my wife and I were sitting side by side. I imagined before us a seat for the Lord and behind us a seat for Satan. My wife and I were players in a larger struggle in which the devil was trying to destroy our marriage.

INTRODUCTION

There is a little yellow booklet by Bill Bright, the founder of Campus Crusade for Christ, called *The Four Spiritual Laws*. It begins with, "God loves you and offers a wonderful plan for your life." I have always believed that to be true. But on those difficult nights, the converse reality occurred to me: "Satan hates you and has a terrible plan for your life." This is not just a logical opposite, it is a biblical truth stated by Jesus and others. Jesus said, "The thief comes only to steal and kill and destroy; I have come that they may have life, and have it to the full" (John 10:10). And the apostle Peter wrote, "Your enemy the devil prowls around like a roaring lion looking for someone to devour" (1 Pet. 5:8).

So the marriage-changing moment occurred for both of us when I acknowledged that my wife was not my enemy. And likewise, she had the same epiphany. We recalled that Jesus said to Peter, "Simon, Simon, Satan has asked to sift all of you as wheat" (Luke 22:31). We realized that Satan desired to grind down our marriage as well.

Again, I do not say this to remove any blame from myself for the evil things I said, only to explain that as long as we saw each other as an enemy, we had a partial picture of reality. This partial picture clouded our understanding of the true significance of our arguments. We were ignorant of the devil's plan to destroy our marriage and were deceived into imagining our full autonomy.

Some people respond with fear to this concept of the devil's plan to use us. During the Reformation in the sixteenth century, people imagined a demon behind every bush. And on the island of Tanna in the South Pacific, where my brother and his family are missionaries, the people are afraid to go in a certain forest for fear of demons. But the Bible assures us, "The one who is in you is greater than the one who is in the world" (1 John 4.4). In other words, we have no need to fear any demonic activity because the Holy Spirit in us is greater than the work of the devil in the world.

Other people receive this concept with guilt. Popular culture, rather than Scripture, has convinced many people that anyone who listens to the devil, is tempted by the devil or is possessed by a demon is evil. The common belief is also that that person is at fault for being influenced. This is clearly not the case in the Bible. Jesus never rebuked or blamed anyone who had been demon-possessed. And the noblest people in Scripture heard directly from Satan, including Peter who tempted Jesus not to go to the cross (see Matt. 16:23). Even Jesus had conversations with the devil and was tempted by him to turn rocks into bread, jump off the pinnacle of the temple and worship him in order to receive power over all the kingdoms of the world (see Matt. 4).

Rather than produce guilt or fear, the realization that the devil desires to use and destroy us ought to be very liberating. It was for my wife's and my marriage. We no longer had to view the other person as the enemy, and we no longer had to view every thought and action as produced from the depth of our own well of evil. That transformative night, rather than seeing me as evil, my wife knew that Satan was using me.

The world makes more sense when we realize that everyone is being used. We have a choice as to how and by whom we will be used. We cannot excuse ourselves from a responsibility to act once we realize we have been used by the devil or another person. Sometimes when we are used, we are truly the victim; but often we also bear the responsibility to identify that we are being used and, whenever possible, to put an end to it by asserting that we will only be used by God.

We can each be used by others, by the devil, and by God. Will you make yourself available as a vessel for use by God alone?

PART ONE

What Does It Mean to Be Used?

1

Ways We Are Used

*"Those who cleanse themselves from the latter will be instruments for special purposes, made holy, **useful** to the Master and prepared to do any good work."*

2 Timothy 2:21, emphasis added

We are always being used. It's not a question of whether to be used, but by whom and for what purpose.

This book will tell many stories of people who were used. Some were used knowingly, others unknowingly. Some were used for good and some for evil. In any case, the common thread is that they acted and someone else's purpose was served. Maybe that purpose was noble, and it all worked out for the best. On the other hand, maybe that purpose was malicious, and the person being used got burned. It's also possible that the person being served was the Self. Once in a while, it can be a treat to serve ourselves, but if it becomes a consistent pattern, then we've got a problem.

Partly this is a book about finding purpose, which is an important aspect of being used by God. But knowing your purpose is only half of the story. The other half is recognizing that whether or not you discover or decide upon your own purpose, others—including malicious people, benevolent people, the devil and God—have a purpose for you as well.

This book will help you understand your purpose as you discover that you are a vessel designed by God for His use. It will help transform your relationships as you discover that they too have the purpose of being used by God.

In my experience as a counselor, I have found that a powerful moment of transformation occurs when people realize that they have been used by others but that their purpose in life is to be used by God. This new understanding of identity has the powerful ability to change actions and mind-sets. Neil Anderson explains the important role that our identity plays in relation to our actions.

> We all live in accordance with our perceived identity. In fact, no one can consistently behave in a way that is inconsistent with how he perceives himself. Your attitudes, actions, responses, and reactions to life's circumstance are determined by your conscious and subconscious self-perception. If you see yourself as the helpless victim of Satan and his schemes, you will live like his victim and be in bondage to his lies. But if you see yourself as the dearly loved and accepted child of God that you really are, you will live like a child of God.[1]

Your identity is how you see yourself. Anderson's point is that how you see yourself affects how you live. I will suggest in this book that the key to transforming your relationships is to see yourself as a vessel for God's use.

Your identity affects your actions. Normally, when we are frustrated, offended or angry, we just react. We act as we see fit, without realizing that a wide array of responses is possible or that others may have acted differently. Say a husband is angry that his wife wastes money on what he thinks are trivial things. Or a mother is terrified that she cannot read her son's text messages once they are deleted. Or an elder in the church is concerned that the board is going to make a terrible decision. Normally, in each of these cases, the husband or the mother or the elder reacts. The husband says he wants separate checking accounts. The mom takes away the cell phone. The elder resigns from the board. But there are other options, and they are options that can transform each relationship. The angry husband, the terrified wife and the concerned elder can pray, "God, how will *You use me* in this situation?"

This book arose from a consistent observation during counseling: relationships are transformed when people ask God how they will be used by Him. It is a biblical concept that addresses the very core of who we are. When we are clear on our identity, we know how to act.

The Bible tells us our purpose and our identity. It says that we are vessels to be used by God. The apostle Paul wrote:

> For God, who said, "Let light shine out of darkness," made his light shine in our hearts to give us the light of the knowledge of the glory of God in the face of Christ. But we have this treasure in jars of clay to show that this all-surpassing power is from God and not from us. We are hard pressed on every side, but not crushed; perplexed, but not in despair; persecuted, but not abandoned; struck down, but not destroyed. We always carry around in our

25

body the death of Jesus, so that the life of Jesus may also be revealed in our body. (2 Cor. 4:6–10)

If we are vessels, then we can conclude several things:

1. We are created.
2. We have purpose.
3. We are meant to carry something.
4. We can be broken.
5. We have a temporary existence on earth.

As Paul references in the passage above, for us to be jars of clay means that we did not arrive on this planet accidently, nor did we create ourselves. We were created by God. He designed us. Every potter who fashions a vessel has a purpose. We do not get to choose our purpose; it is assigned to us by God. What are we meant to carry? Paul explains that we carry with us the death of Jesus. In other words, we carry the truth and consequences of the gospel. We formerly carried the curse of sin, but now we carry the message and evidence of new life. The prophet Jeremiah used clay vessels as object lessons for the Israelite people (see Jer. 18–19). One of his lessons was that clay can be fashioned when it is soft; but when it hardens, it can be dashed to pieces. As vessels, we also can be broken, and our brokenness can be caused either willingly or unwillingly. When we humble ourselves and repent, we willingly break ourselves. But when we are proud, God often allows an occasion to break us against our sinful will.

The realization that I can be a vessel used by God, by others and by the devil was life changing for me. It transformed my relationship with my wife and then began to transform the way I look at my other relationships as well. I hope that, as you read, you enjoy the same experience of finding hope and purpose as a vessel for God's use.

As vessels, when we act, we serve someone's purpose. That could be good news or bad news, depending on who's using you and for what purpose. When someone uses you, you often feel as if you've been taken advantage of—even more so if you question the other person's motive. Most of all, you feel offended when you find out you've been used unknowingly. Ironically, however, sometimes it is truly a joy to be used. We are all used in different ways:

- When you are used unconsciously, it's manipulation.
- When you are used consciously but unwillingly, it's slavery.
- When you are used consciously and willingly, it's a joyful service.

Used Unconsciously

The devil often uses people who are unaware of that fact. So do cult leaders, many serial killers, thieves, masters of manipulation, drug addicts, alcoholics and psychological bullies. All of us, in fact, are guilty of using others for our own gain. Let's look at a few examples.

In Robert Penn Warren's book *All the King's Men*, we read of Willie Stark, who, without his knowledge, was used by his political opponents. Stark was talked into running for governor of Louisiana by people who he thought shared his political views and supported him. But in reality, Joe Harrison, the incumbent governor, needed a dummy candidate to split the vote for his opponent. Worried he was going to lose the election, Harrison looked for someone who was unlikely to win to run against him to take away votes from his likely rival. The plan backfired, however, in a later election. Stark came to power and brought sweeping reforms, much

27

to the chagrin of the people who originally helped get him interested in politics. Eventually, Stark came to realize that he had been used by his opponents.

Used Consciously but Unwillingly

Perpetrators of sexual assault and violent crime use people who are conscious of the fact but unwilling. So do thieves, extortionists, smugglers and people in authority. During WWII the Nazis used people unwillingly for medical experiments. Millions of Africans were used unwillingly as slaves during the colonial period. The concept of "being used" can be frightening, because each of us has experienced a time when we were used, manipulated or enslaved.

In Genesis we read the amazing story of Joseph, who was sold into slavery by his brothers (see chapters 37–45). Because they were jealous of their father's preferential love for Joseph, they threw him in a pit out of vengeance. They then realized that, in addition to getting rid of their brother, they could also profit by selling him as a slave and could avoid being guilty of bloodshed. Joseph's brothers sold him into slavery; and eventually he ended up as the household slave of a man named Potiphar, a ruler in Egypt. There, he proved himself a trustworthy worker.

Things went well until Joseph was falsely accused of sexual harassment by Potiphar's wife (she was angry that he'd fled when she'd tried to seduce him) and thrown in jail. But because Joseph was able to interpret dreams, he was summoned by Pharaoh to explain a dream. Joseph correctly interpreted the dream and then rose in power. Because of a famine back home, Joseph's brothers came looking for help, which landed them in Joseph's court. At first they did not recognize him. When they did, they assumed that he had the power and inclination to kill them. But Joseph uttered this incredible affirmation in the sovereignty of God, "It was not you who sent me here, but God" (Gen. 45:8).

Most of us are mindful of the natural ways in which we are used. We can see that Joseph's brothers used him. Potiphar's wife used him. Even Pharaoh used him. But Joseph was sensitive to see that behind the scenes of the natural world, he was being used by God in a greater way. Joseph said, "You intended to harm me, but God intended it for good to accomplish what is now being done, the saving of many lives" (50:20). Joseph took consolation in knowing that even if a man convinces himself he is using others for his own purposes, this is merely an illusion of control, for in reality we are being used by God or Satan in a grander scheme. This conviction enabled Joseph to thrive amidst enemies. In the pit, he realized that his brothers were not his true enemies; he also knew that human beings could not be his strongest ally. Joseph was determined to be used by God as an instrument of salvation during the time of famine, even if it meant enduring the ruse of other people using him for their selfish purposes.

Because "we know that in all things God works for the good" (Rom. 8:28), we know that He can do for us what He did for Joseph. No matter what situation we are in, God can use it for good, even if someone else intended evil.

Used Consciously and Willingly

Despite the frightening examples of people being used unconsciously and unwillingly, we need not fear. God gives us an invitation to be used by Him, and we can be conscious and willing participants. The moment we realize that we have been used by others but can now be used by God is liberating: it gives us protection from the past, purpose for the future and joy for the present.

Being used by God inevitably means giving something up. We are told in Philippians:

> Each of you should look not only to your own interests, but also to the interests of others. Your attitude should be the same as that of Christ Jesus: Who, being in very nature God, did not consider equality with God something to be grasped, but made himself nothing, taking the very nature of a servant, being made in human likeness. (2:4–7)

The phrase "made himself nothing" has caused much theological debate. The Greek word is *kenosis*, and that is the concept by which the "emptying of Christ" has come to be known. But of what did Christ empty himself? Various answers have been offered.[2] Perhaps Jesus emptied himself of the three defining characteristics of God: omniscience (all-knowing), omnipresence (all-present) and omnipotence (all-powerful). But for Christ to empty himself of these things means He would no longer be God, and the Bible says, "God was pleased to have all his fullness dwell in him" (Col. 1:19). Many theologians have suggested that Jesus emptied himself of the "independen exercise of his divine attributes." But when did Christ ever do anything independently of the Father? I think it is best to understand that Christ emptied himself of His glory: His fame, reputation and the honor due His name. He emptied himself of His rights: the right to be worshiped, feared, respected and exalted. By emptying himself of His rights, He was able to be used by God consciously and willingly.

We are encouraged in Philippians to have the same attitude as Christ. Christ's attitude was a willingness to give up all things for the purpose of carrying out the Father's will. We are called to practice *kenosis*, the emptying of our rights. By practicing our own emptying, we are able to be used by God for the benefit of others.

Some people give up their glory, or their right to be honored, unwillingly. When a pastor is accused of sexual abuse and is defrocked, he loses his right to be highly esteemed, which is no honorable sacrifice. A high profile athlete may end his career early due to an injury and thus give up his glory unwillingly.

Others give up their glory willingly but reluctantly. We often hear of politicians who end their careers "for personal reasons." Often these personal reasons coincide with highly publicized controversies but not always. In the case where the abdication of glory truly is for the benefit of one's family, it is more commendable, yet still less sacrificial than the emptying Jesus exemplified.

Christ willingly, sacrificially and joyfully gave up his right to be glorified. We can have this same attitude when emptying ourselves. When we do, we make ourselves available to be used by God.

2

A Prayer to Be Used

"You've a lot to learn about trucks, little Thomas. They are silly things and must be kept in their place. After pushing them about here for a few weeks you'll know about as much about them as Edward. Then you'll be Really Useful Engine."

—Rev. W.V. Awdry

I began watching *Thomas the Tank Engine* films with my kids years ago, and it doesn't take more than two episodes to figure out one of the story's core values: usefulness. Thomas is commended repeatedly for being a useful engine, and this puts a smile on his face. It is our destiny and our purpose to be used by God. When we awaken each day with a prayer to be used by God, we alter the course of that day and give it purpose. More importantly, when we face each relational difficulty with a prayer to be used by God, we alter the course of that relationship and find our purpose within it. Thinking of ourselves as a vessel for God's use transforms our lives.

The poem below, entitled the "Prayer of Saint Francis," illustrates this transformation. It is a prayer to be used as God's instrument. The poet expresses the concept of this book—a person who desires to be used by God.

> Lord, make me an instrument of your peace.
> Where there is hatred, let me sow love;
> where there is injury, pardon;
> where there is doubt, faith;
> where there is despair, hope;
> where there is darkness, light;
> and where there is sadness, joy.
>
> O Divine Master, grant that I may not so much seek
> to be consoled as to console;
> to be understood as to understand;
> to be loved as to love.
> For it is in giving that we receive;
> it is in pardoning that we are pardoned;
> and it is in dying that we are born to eternal life. Amen

Used on Purpose

In *The Purpose Driven Life*, Rick Warren addresses a question on the minds of millions of people today and throughout history: What is my purpose in life? He explains that the primary reason each of us exists is to be used by God. Warren writes, "You were made by God and for God—and until you understand that, life will never make sense."[1] Though there are unique aspects about each person's purpose that no book could address, there are some universal answers to the question of the purpose of our lives. Warren suggests three biblical concepts that help us understand our purpose as vessels for use by God:

1. You discover your identity and purpose through a relationship with Jesus Christ.
2. God was thinking of you long before you ever thought about him. His purpose for your life pre-dates your conception. He planned it before you existed *without your input*! You may choose your career, your spouse, your hobbies, and many other parts of your life, but you don't get to choose your purpose.
3. The purpose of your life fits into a much larger, cosmic purpose that God has designed for eternity.[2]

Not only does God have a purpose for each person; He has a purpose for the whole universe. Warren writes, "The ultimate goal of the universe is to show the glory of God. It is the reason for everything that exists, including you. God made it *all* for his glory."[3] In other words, the primary purpose for the world and everything in it is to be used by God. Paul makes this clear in Colossians 1:16: "For by him all things were created: things in heaven and on earth, visible and in-visible, whether thrones or powers or rulers or authorities; all things were created by him and for him."

We know that we can be used by others. And we know that we can be used by the devil. We can be used unwillingly and unconsciously. But the life-changing moment for Christians is when we realize that we can—and determine that we will—be used by God. Warren encourages, "Living for God's glory is the greatest achievement we can accomplish with our lives."[4] It is our purpose to be used by God. And with faith in God's goodness, wisdom and power, we know that being used is not always a bad thing, depending on who's using you.

PART TWO

Used by Others

3

Use(less)

"Remember that the most beautiful things in the world are the most useless; peacocks and lilies for instance."

—John Ruskin in *Stones of Venice*

No doubt there are elderly people today who think the only way younger generations will find them useful is to inherit their money. Some elderly people must wonder how else they could be used. But we all have information, gathered over a lifetime of experiences, that can be useful to future generations. There is no person who is useless to God, regardless of age or abilities.

Ruth: The Mother-in-Law

In the biblical story of Ruth, we read of a woman named Naomi who believed she was useless (see Ruth 1). She had two married sons—Mahlon (whose name means "sickly") and Kilion (whose name means "cry baby"). Both sons died and left Ruth with two daughters-in-law. Naomi was a Jewish woman, but her daughters-in-law were from Moab. She said to them:

> Return home, my daughters. Why would you come with me? Am I going to have any more sons, who could become your husbands? Return home, my daughters; I am too old to have another husband. Even if I thought there was still hope for me—even if I had a husband tonight and then gave birth to sons—would you wait until they grew up? Would you remain unmarried for them? No, my daughters. It is more bitter for me than for you, because the LORD's hand has gone out against me! (Ruth 1:11–13)

Naomi believed that the only way she could have value to these other women was to produce sons for them to marry; and since that was not going to happen, she resolved that she was worthless and should be alone. From the rest of the story, we learn that her daughter-in-law Ruth followed her back to Bethlehem, lived with her and married a man named Boaz who provided for both women. From that information, it still doesn't sound like Naomi was used. To be sure, Ruth was used by God to provide for Naomi, but was the older woman useless? Not at all. Naomi was a wise woman—behind every decision that Ruth made was Naomi's sage advice. Naomi instructed Ruth how to ask for food from Boaz, how to build a relationship with him and how to get him to notice her. Though Naomi was poor and old, she was not useless because she had information God used for the benefit of those around her.

If for some reason you have doubted whether God can use you for some noble purpose, I admonish you to look to Naomi for encouragement. You are not useless. Paul explained to the young Timothy how the young are at a disadvantage with regard to their usefulness.

> In a large house there are articles not only of gold and silver, but also of wood and clay; some are for noble purposes and some for ignoble. If a man cleanses himself from the latter, he will be an instrument for noble purposes, made holy, useful to the Master and prepared to do any good work. Flee the evil desires of youth, and pursue righteousness, faith, love and peace, along with those who call on the Lord out of a pure heart. (2 Tim. 2:20–22)

Usefulness to God depends upon the preparation of the vessel and whether it is clean. In this sense, youthfulness is a disadvantage because of immature passions and desires. Age is often regarded highly in Scripture, and one advantage mentioned here is the growing ability to resist the temptation to sin as we grow in our faith. The mature who have overcome temptation have thereby become all the more useful to God.

Often our feeling of uselessness results from our failure to see in ourselves what others see. We all perceive ourselves differently than the people around us. One time I went to the bank and noticed that everyone was smiling at me—some nervously, others in a charming way, and still others trying to hide the fact that they were smiling. This was very bizarre, but I just went on with my next chore and visited the pharmacy. There too, people smiled and giggled as subtly as they could. I knew something I was unaware of had to be obvious to others. So I drove home, burst through the door and yelled, "What's funny about me?!" My wife said, "Could it be the tiara that Leah made out of pipe cleaners and put on your head before you left?" That was it! The tiara was so light I had completely forgotten about it. I trust that when I was at the bank and the pharmacy, people said to themselves, "That guy lost some bet with his five-year-old."

Our hope in being used by God is not to overcome the disparity between how we see ourselves and how others see us but instead to know how God sees us. In every case, He sees a person He can use.

4

Used Up

*"A great secret of success is to go through life as a man
who never gets used up."*
—*Albert Schweitzer*

Albert Schweitzer had every reason to believe that he
had reached the height of usefulness—and then he
found a completely new place in life. At age twenty-four he completed a PhD in theology and gave birth to a
new (albeit subversive) movement in critical biblical studies.
Following that, he became an accomplished church organ-
ist. Due to his love of music, he began a hobby of rebuilding
organs in churches throughout Europe. As if these achieve-
ments weren't enough, when he was thirty-seven, he became
a medical doctor and moved to Africa as a missionary. The
beauty of life is that we never know what tomorrow holds.
Each day adds the promise of a new way to be used by God.
We are never used up.

Fay: The Grandma

My first teaching experience in the church was a ten-week evangelism class. I had a handful of students, most of them elderly. They were gracious and supportive. They said they liked having a young teacher in their class. I could see plainly from the expressions on their faces that they thought the topic of evangelism was irrelevant. One elderly woman named Fay was confined to a wheelchair. She said what the others were feeling: "I can't evangelize. I don't go anywhere, and I don't work. I think I'll have to leave the work of evangelism to the younger people." She wasn't defiant or argumentative in her tone. She was just making sure I was aware of the problem. So I asked her, "Do you know anyone who is not a Christian?" She said, "My daughter. Her husband. My granddaughter." I asked her where they lived. She said, "With me." As it turned out, in addition to those family members living in her home, her son, her other daughter and her other son-in-law also lived next door. In other words, six non-Christian family members lived *right next to her*! And yet, because of her age, she had concluded that she had no work of evangelism left in her. I suggested to Fay that she start small. She could pray for her family, and she could invite them to church.

Over the next few weeks in our class, she did invite her daughter. Her daughter, in turn, invited her husband and daughter. In a year's time, all six members of Fay's family accepted Christ and became integral members of our church. All this resulted from the simple prayer and invitation from a woman who thought she could not be used as an evangelist. But the transforming moment came when Fay said, "I can be used to bring others to Christ."

The Psalms promise that the godly aged are never "used up." Psalm 92:12–14 says, "The righteous will flourish like a palm tree, they will grow like a cedar of Lebanon; planted in the house of the LORD, they will flourish in the courts of our God. They will still bear fruit in old age, they will stay fresh and green."

The aged are not the only ones inclined to think they are used up. Joni Eareckson Tada became a quadriplegic after a diving accident at the age of eighteen. She could have assumed that her life was no longer useful to God; but she became a noted painter (using her teeth to hold the brush), author, speaker and disabilities advocate. Shortly after the accident, she determined that she was not "used up." Joni writes in her memoir:

> Once again I desperately wanted to kill myself. Here I was, trapped in this canvas cocoon. I couldn't move anything except my head. Why on earth should a person be forced to live out such a dreary existence? But once again, there was no way for me to commit suicide. This frustration was also unbearable.[1]

Though Joni initially entertained the thought of suicide, she had a moment of transformation when she realized that no matter what her condition, she could be used as a vessel by God. She discovered that each day has purpose, and that alone is enough. Eareckson says, "Who cared how I responded? God cared. Did I really have the right to complain about my injured face? No. My body was not my own: it was God's to do with as he pleased. He bought it with his own Son's blood."[2]

If anyone has the legitimate right to tell others that they can be useful to God, no matter their physical condition, it is Joni Eareckson Tada. Her message is that we must overcome the selfish inclination to make each day meaningful on our own terms. We don't get to pick the purpose for which we live. It has been assigned to us, it is the same for all and it can be accomplished by every living person. Joni explains it this way:

> I really don't mind the inconvenience of being paralyzed if my faithfulness to God while in this wheelchair will bring glory to him. Have you ever considered the potential glory your life can give to God if, in your "wheelchair," you remain faithful?[3]

When I lived in the country, our closest neighbor (a mile away) was a great-grandmother named Mary. I visited her one time and was touched by a handwritten chart she had on her wall. She had a family tree of all her living relatives that she informed me she used as a daily prayer guide. Each day she prayed for everyone in her family. Trust me, this took some time, because she had over one hundred names on this elaborate chart! Even though Mary was in her nineties, she was conscious of the unique way she could be used by God each day.

Regardless of your age, your physical condition, your mental abilities or the persuasiveness of your speech, you can be used by God as well. Even if you spend much of your time alone or at home, there are people in your life to whom you can radiate the light of Christ. You are not used up.

5

Use(ful)

*"There is nothing so useless as doing efficiently
that which should not be done at all."*

—Peter Drucker

When I was a teenager, a friend invited me to his mother's home for dinner. We were waiting and chatting as we watched her cook. Then she put a wet towel on the table but didn't clean anything. She waited a moment, started cooking and said, "Some people believe in doing everything yourself. I'm not like that. I think you should let the people around you help." I agreed. My friend agreed. She still didn't get her point across. My friend helped translate, pointing to the towel, "That's her tactful way of saying 'Make yourself useful.'"

"Make yourself useful." That's something we do. It's active and self-directed. You decide when and how and where to make yourself useful. From a biblical perspective, making yourself useful is often presumptuous. It can often mean that you know what is needed and that you are the right person for the job.

I have a terrible habit of presuming that I can make myself useful. For instance, when I was painting my house and my electric paint sprayer broke, my first thought was to disassemble it. Then I was struck by the offensive pride behind that idea. I thought, *Dan, you don't know anything about these sprayers; you're not a paint sprayer repair man.* While an adventurous and independent spirit can be helpful and admirable, when left unchecked, we can start believing we ourselves are the primary solution to every problem, which is an offense to God. King Nebuchadnezzar exhibited this presumptuous attitude when he said, "Is not this the great Babylon I have built as the royal residence, by my mighty power and for the glory of my majesty?" (Dan. 4:30). God was not impressed. As punishment for this self-praise, the king was doomed to insanity and living like a wild animal for seven years.

Paul encouraged, "Do not think of yourself more highly than you ought, but rather think of yourself with sober judgment" (Rom. 12:3). Such humble thinking will prevent us from viewing ourselves as God's gift to mankind. We honor God with a humble attitude; but we also protect ourselves, for "Pride goes before destruction, a haughty spirit before a fall" (Prov. 16:18).

"Used," on the other hand, is passive, yet it's participatory. It is other-directed. That means being used can be both good and bad. If you are used by someone else for evil or for selfish gain, it's a tragedy, and we need to identify when this is happening so that we can avoid these situations. But if you are being used by God, it is a fulfilling pleasure, a great joy and a worthy purpose in life. When you are used, rather than making yourself useful, you say to God that He is the primary solution to every problem and that you are willing to be a part of His design.

Henry Blackaby and Claude King warn of the difference between acting presumptuously and responding to an invitation from God to act. In *Experiencing God* they write:

> We do not sit down and dream what we want to do for God and then call God in to help us accomplish it. Who delivered the children of Israel from Egypt? Moses or God? God did. Did Moses ever try to take matters about the children of Israel into his own hands? Yes. Moses began to assert himself in behalf of his own people. What might have happened if Moses had tried to deliver the children of Israel through a human approach? Thousands and thousands would have been slain. Moses tried to take Israelite matters into his own hands. That cost him 40 years of exile in Midian working as a shepherd (and reorienting his life to God-centered living). Why do we not realize that it is always best to do things God's way? We cause some of the wreck and ruin in our churches because we have a plan. We implement the plan and get out of it only what we can do. God (Jesus) is head over the body—the church. He will accomplish more in six months through a people yielded to him than we could do in 60 years without Him.[1]

To be used by God means to respond to what God is doing. It does not mean that we make ourselves useful by deciding on our own accord what we will do. When you make yourself useful, you act independently. But when you are used by God, you are dependent upon Him and upon hearing His will. Making yourself useful is reminiscent of the adage, "Don't just stand there, do something!" But is there value in just doing something? People who wait for God's direction understand the wisdom of the phrase, "Don't just do something, stand there!" Sometimes our desire to make ourselves useful gets in the way of being used by God. You can be a vessel for God's use as you look for where He is at work and make yourself available.

6

(Ab)used

"I know we have won many a soul through pleasure. All the same it is His invention, not ours: all our research so far has not enabled us to produce one. All we can do is encourage the humans to take the pleasures which our Enemy has produced at times, or in ways, or in degrees which He has forbidden."

—*Screwtape in C.S. Lewis'* The Screwtape Letters[1]

The most visible way the devil uses us is through the abuse of pleasure. Though God created every kind of pleasure, each can easily be abused. Since it can be tempting to fall into abuse or be abused by others in their pursuit of pleasure, it is easy to become hopeless and think we have lost our usefulness to God. The apostle Paul addresses people who have fallen to a variety of abuses: "Neither the sexually immoral, nor idolaters, nor adulterers, nor men who practice homosexuality, nor thieves, nor the greedy, nor drunkards, nor revilers, nor swindlers will inherit the kingdom of God. And such were some of you." (1 Cor. 6:9–11, ESV).

That last phrase, though not very flattering or encouraging, is actually an understatement. Not only were some of us abusers and abused, but we are all guilty! Paul, however, follows that warning with a beautiful three letter word, "But...," he continues, "But you were washed, you were sanctified, you were justified in the name of the Lord Jesus Christ and by the Spirit of our God." (1 Cor. 6:11). Whatever name you gave yourself when you were used (liar, slut, loser, drunkard, dirtbag, scum) you don't have to keep it. Now you can be used in a new way. Your body can be redeemed and renewed. Though it was once used by others, your body can now be used by God to give him glory.

Sara: The Object

Sara looked at a blank piece of paper when I asked her to write down a short list of ways to describe herself. She stared for a few minutes, so I stepped out of the room, thinking she was embarrassed and needed to be alone. When I came back it was still blank. We discussed her background, and a tragic story unfolded. She is a twenty-year-old mother who has been pregnant three times. She was sexually abused as a child, raped as a teenager and then physically abused by her first boyfriend. It became clear to me why the paper was blank. She didn't know who she was; she only knew how others saw her. And that list only had one thing on it—a sexual object. She had come to believe that this was the only way to describe herself. She was a thing with one purpose—to be used by men.

On another occasion Sara came into my office crying. I asked her what was on her mind, and she said, "I am a ho girl" (a prostitute). She confessed that she had hooked up with a guy the night before for a one-night stand. It was the first

52

time in her life she had done such a thing, but eight hours later she was ready to declare that this was her new identity.

She had a new name for herself. Imagine the power of this name. It would now define her, based on what she had done the night before. She admitted that because of her new name it was inevitable that she would do this again since that is what ho girls do. Her future was paved, and her future actions excusable all because of a new name—Ho Girl.

Dulcinea: Sweet Thing

Miguel de Cervantes' classic *Don Quixote* was adapted into the Broadway musical and film, *Man of La Mancha*. The seemingly crazy Don Quixote knows that every noble knight has a fair lady, so he searches for the perfect maiden. He arrives in a poor, insignificant town and turns his attention to a woman of ill repute. But that is not what he sees. Instead, the man who sees himself as a valuable knight sees a woman who is so pure and noble he does not deserve her. They sing:

DON QUIXOTE
Sweet lady . . . fair virgin . . .
I dare not gaze full upon thy countenance
Lest I be blinded by beauty. But I implore
Thee - speak once thy name.

ALDONZA
Aldonza.

DON QUIXOTE
My lady jests.

ALDONZA
Aldonza!

DON QUIXOTE
The name of a kitchen-scullion . . . or perhaps my
lady's serving-maid?

ALDONZA
I told you my name! Now get out of the way.

DON QUIXOTE
Did my lady think to put me to a test?
Ah, sweet sovereign of my captive heart. I shall
not fail thee, for I know . . .

I have dreamed thee too long,
Never seen thee or touched thee.
But known thee with all of my heart.
Half a prayer, half a song,
Thou hast always been with me,
Though we have been always apart.

Dulcinea . . . Dulcinea . . .
I see heaven when I see thee, Dulcinea,
And thy name is like a prayer
An angel whispers . . . Dulcinea . . . Dulcinea!

If I reach out to thee,
Do not tremble and shrink
From the touch of my hand on thy hair.
Let my fingers but see
Thou art warm and alive,
And no phantom to fade in the air.

Dulcinea . . . Dulcinea . . .
I have sought thee, sung thee,
Dreamed thee, Dulcinea!

> Now I've found thee,
> And the world shall know thy glory,
> Dulcinea . . . Dulcinea!

The name "Dulcinea" can be translated "sweet thing." To the woman and to the people she knew in the town, she was anything but a sweet and fair virgin, but such was the way Don Quixote beheld her. And, perhaps in time, having heard it enough from her pursuer, it would be the way she could see herself. When called by the name Dulcinea, the woman was confronted with a crisis of identity. How would she see herself? The way her townspeople view her (as Aldonza)? Or the way Don Quixote saw her (as Dulcinea)?

This crisis of identity leads to a decision of how one's body will be used. Will Dulcinea's body be used by men to satisfy their passions, or will her body be used for honor in a holy marriage?

Don Quixote is an image of Christ, and Aldonza is an image of the church. What the world sees as a prostitute, Christ sees as Dulcinea, a sweet thing. Paul writes, "As for you, you were dead in your transgressions and sins, in which you used to live when you followed the ways of this world and of the ruler of the kingdom of the air, the spirit who is now at work in those who are disobedient. All of us also lived among them at one time, gratifying the cravings of our sinful nature and following its desires and thoughts. Like the rest, we were by nature objects of wrath. But because of his great love for us, God, who is rich in mercy, made us alive with Christ" (Eph. 2:1–5). While it is true that each of us at one point has been as shameful as Aldonza, that is not the way Christ sees us. We are not objects of wrath. We are not dead in our sins. We are alive in Christ. We are His bride, beautifully adorned, and being made ready for our wedding feast with Him.

How God Sees You

Imagine the transforming power this truth has for how your body will be used. If Don Quixote could transform Aldonza into Dulcinea by giving her a new name and thereby a new identity, how does the fact that Christ has prepared for you a new name transform your identity? Jesus promises each Christian, "I will also give him a white stone with a new name written on it, known only to him who receives it" (Rev. 2:17).

In the ancient world stones were used as ballots. The name of the person you voted for would be written on the stone. Sometimes the stones were painted different colors for different purposes. That's because these same stones could be used to ostracize someone from the community. The word "ostracize," in fact, comes from the Greek word for a broken piece of pottery, which could also be used for voting. So when Jesus says He has prepared for us a white stone with the writing of a new name, He is promising to vote in favor of us. He is casting a yes vote to include us in the community.

As a Christian, your identity has changed. Paul writes, "If anyone is in Christ, he is a new creation; the old has gone, the new has come!" (2 Cor. 5:17).

May the new name by which Christ knows you give you a secure identity so that your body will be used for a new purpose—no longer for the use of other people, because that is not who you are. Your body is a vessel for God.

Used in a New Way with Old Relationships

People who grow up in dysfunctional or abusive relationships will eventually need to redefine the purpose of those relationships if they are going to be successful. One of the young adults in our church named Greg is a good example. His mother struggled with mental illness, which led to controlling behaviors, obsessive compulsions and cycles of manic or depressive phases. Though his family was slow to diagnose the problem, eventually they realized Greg's mother had a mental disorder. Greg was aware that his situation was abnormal and this enabled him to extend grace toward his mother for her condition, rather than become consumed with frustration or anger. Nevertheless, there were some difficult times back when Greg was a teenager. His mother reacted in unpredictable ways; she made demands that seemed unreasonable to him. At times he felt the only way to survive was to run away.

But when Greg became an adult, he asked himself the transforming questions that are the focus of this book:

- "How does God intend to use me?"
- "What is the purpose of this relationship?"
- "Why has God placed me in this family?"
- "What is my role in my mother's life?"

These are life-changing questions, and they enabled Greg to break away from the cycle of dysfunction. By asking these questions, Greg was able to distance himself from the problems in his family. Then he was able to return, somewhat as an outsider with a more objective view. (He wasn't an outsider to the family, as if he had rejected or abandoned them, but an outsider to the dysfunction.) He came to his parent's home not as a victim or a child but as someone who offered something. He achieved a strong sense of purpose in reentering his childhood home. His answers to the above questions were based on his identity in Christ:

- "The purpose of this relationship is for me to be the image of Christ to my parents."
- "God intends to use me as an instrument of grace to those around me."
- "My role as an adult child is to become more like Christ, and to aid others in doing so as well."

Finding Purpose in Relationships Helps Heal (Ab)use

In one way or another, most of us have been abused, whether in the form of sexual abuse, physical abuse, verbal abuse or neglect. And there are more subtle and pervasive forms of abuse such as power and intimidation. A powerful step in overcoming the experience of abuse is the realization that we have been used by others and can be used by God. This provides a narrative, or an explanatory framework, to make sense of why we experienced what we did and where we go now. If you have found yourself used and abused by others, you have an opportunity to find new purpose. Formerly, others defined your purpose and defined how you could be used. Now you can choose to be used in a new way, and by a new Person. That Person, the all-loving and all-knowing God, designed you and your body. Are you going to let others define how you will be used, or will you allow God to define your purpose?

7

Used to Enable

*"For a brief moment I deserted you, but with great compassion
I will gather you."*

Isaiah 54:7, ESV

In the verse above from Isaiah, we read how God rescued Israel from her own sin and punishment—but not too soon. When we rescue someone too soon, it's called "enabling." One common way we are used by others is as their enabler. If you've ever watched the TV series *Intervention*, you know it's easy to identify the drug or alcohol abuser who needs to be rescued. It's equally easy to identify their enablers. Behind every abuser there is an enabler. The enabler rescues them time and time again by supplying food, money, shelter, etc. Enablers are being used. Consider the following story of an enabler used by her daughter.

Susan: The Enabling Parent

Susan, like many other parents, is the mother of boomerang kids (adult children she sent out but they came back). She came to me asking for advice about how to deal with her grown daughter who lives with her. Her daughter, Jessica, watches cartoons—while wearing sweatpants and eating Cheerios—in the afternoons. It is absolutely clear that Susan loves her daughter and even enjoys her company at home, but she knows that Jessica is not on a path to maturity. She is not looking for work or progressing in school, so there is little indication that her life will be different ten years from now.

Susan has a dilemma: she wants her daughter to grow up, but she also wants her to feel loved. Susan knows that helping Jessica grow up probably means giving her the ultimatum that she has to find some worthwhile way to occupy her time or move out. When Susan considers giving her daughter such an ultimatum, she is flooded with many of her own objections and questions. She thinks: *Jessica will probably throw a fit and be mad at me. She'll suffer if I kick her out because she won't have anywhere to go and I'll feel terrible.* These concerns are driven by the desire to be liked, but we are often equally driven by the desire to have power, so Susan expressed other concerns: *How am I going to make her get a job? What if she doesn't do what I say?*

Susan has made it easy for Jessica to live her current lifestyle. Susan is not primarily responsible for her daughter's actions; Jessica is. But Susan is enabling Jessica to develop self-defeating behaviors. So Susan isn't sure what to do. What she doesn't realize is that she is already being used. We are always being used. It's not a question of whether to be used, but by whom we will be used and for what purpose. Jessica is using her mother to enable her to live a lifestyle that could ultimately destroy her.

Susan reached the point of transformation when she asked herself these defining questions:

- "How does God want to use me now in this situation?"
- "How and by whom have I been used so far?"
- "What is the purpose of this relationship?"
- "What is the role of a parent in the life of an adult child? Is it primarily to be friends? To feel loved? To make the other person feel loved? To make the other person happy? To provide for the other person's needs?"

Boundaries

One of the key issues that Susan has to confront is boundaries. As an enabler, she has allowed her daughter to maintain a self-defeating lifestyle. She was so afraid of causing pain in someone else's life that she was unable to say no to her daughter without feeling guilty. She feared that Jessica would lash out in anger if she kicked her out of the home or if she refused to provide for her. Even more keenly, she felt miserable about causing any unnecessary suffering for her daughter. As long as it was within her power to alleviate some pain for Jessica, she would do it. As long as her daughter needed a place to stay and she could provide it, she would oblige.

But was her behavior loving? Susan came to me because she was conflicted and knew there was something wrong with what she was doing. She knew that the Bible says, "He who spares the rod hates his son, but he who loves him is careful to discipline him" (Prov. 13:24). Though her daughter was certainly beyond the age of spanking, she knew that even as an adult Jessica needed some discipline, and she was failing to provide it.

So here is how Susan answered those questions:

- "I am an agent of God in disciplining my children."
- "My role is to be the image of Christ in their lives."
- "I have been used to enable my daughter, but I will now be used by God to mature her."

In their book *Boundaries*, Henry Cloud and John Townsend explain the importance of establishing boundaries not only for our own protection but out of love for others. Cloud and Townsend explain, "Boundaries are anything that helps to differentiate you from someone else, or shows where you begin and end."[1]

Some people think that establishing a boundary is selfish and unloving. But Cloud and Townsend are convinced that boundaries improve and save relationships. They ask, "How many marriages could have been saved if one spouse had followed through with the threat of 'if you don't stop drinking' (or 'coming home at midnight,' or 'hitting me' or 'yelling at the kids'), I will leave until you get some treatment!"[2]

If Susan, the enabling mother above, establishes boundaries with her child/adult daughter, she increases the likelihood of Jessica's success and the success of their relationship. But when I mentioned this to her, she was unsure. She asked the same question that Cloud and Townsend address: "Don't boundaries turn us from other-centeredness to self-centeredness? The answer is no. *Appropriate boundaries actually increase our ability to care about others*."[3] That's because caring for others means doing what is in their best interest, and drawing a boundary for someone may be the most caring thing you can do.

Not surprisingly, Susan discovered that not only did she enable her daughter to have self-defeating behavior, she also had an enabling relationship with her husband, Glen. She rarely expressed disagreement with her husband and chose to comply with his demands on how to spend money, where to go on vacation, how to spend their leisure time and even what job she should have. Coming to grips with how she had been used to enable meant that she had to consider these questions again:

- How will God use me in this relationship?
- What is the purpose of this relationship?

Susan's answer was, "I am one of God's instruments in discipling my husband. God can use me to help him learn cooperation." Enabling her husband's controlling behavior meant Susan was missing an important way for her to be used by God. God is always at work discipling his children and fashioning them into His image. Susan is one of God's children, and she has a role to play in God's work. Long before Susan came into her husband's life, God was at work chipping away at Glen's controlling disposition. It is not Susan's job to be the first voice or the only voice that reveals Glen's propensity to be overbearing. God has already been speaking to his conscience about this through the Holy Spirit. Just as I am certain that the devil speaks to us, I am also convinced that God speaks, and God does a better job at getting through. The Bible promises, "The one who is in you is greater than the one who is in the world" (1 John 4:4). Susan must have faith that God was at work in Glen's life before she came around and that God will continue that work. Her role, therefore, is to echo the voice of God that is already speaking to Glen's conscience. That is how she can be used by God rather than used to enable.

8

Used for Other's Gain

"Nor [will] swindlers inherit the kingdom of God."
1 Corinthians 6:10

Recently, my twenty-one-year-old son bought a car from a dealership. Sonny arrived at the dealership at 5:00 p.m., but he had to leave for work at 6:00 p.m. He chose the car he wanted and agreed on a price but wasn't able to settle everything before his departure time. The salesman said to him, "Get on the phone and call in sick. You can't go to work. This is the deal of a lifetime. You don't want to miss it. This is worth missing a day of work for." Now I'd say the salesman overplayed his card. It's sometimes easy to see when we are being used by someone for their financial gain; and even though my son was inexperienced at car buying, he could tell that claim was just a little over the top. But it's not always so easy to see when we're being taken advantage of.

Jack: The Loan Shark

When my wife and I were young, we had our eye on a house we wanted to purchase. We had a condo we wanted to keep as an investment, but we wanted to move into the house. The loan officers we approached told us we were very close to qualifying for the loan. "You're almost qualified," one officer told us. We just needed to make twice as much money.

Then one lender named Jack promised us the loan. We filled out piles of paperwork, and as the date of escrow approached, the loan officer asked us for proof that our condo was about to sell. Though our conversation was on the phone, I could feel him wink as he said, "You have a promise from someone to buy it, right?" He couldn't see the problem with fabricating a piece of paper in order to accomplish both his and our goals. But we figured out why he was able to do what no one else could; he had misrepresented us to the lender. Ultimately, we decided to sell the condo rather than lie. I remember the sickening thought that I had been used for someone else's gain.

No doubt you have a similar story of someone using you for their purpose, whether it was for money, reputation, pleasure, information, etc. There is a sense of violation. The only mitigation for the disgust is to realize that you too are guilty. I too have used others for my gain. We have all used others for our gain.

Balaam: The Mercenary Prophet

In the biblical account of Balaam we read of a man who was used both by enemies and by God (see Num. 22–24). There was a king named Balak who reigned over a neighboring nation called Moab. He conceived of human beings as independent agents who could do whatever they wished. He hired a prophet named Balaam, who he promised to richly reward if he would curse Israel. Balaam was willing to take the cash and to curse Israel if necessary, but he was wiser in his view of human nature than Balak. The prophet knew that humans could be used by God, man and the devil, so Balaam gave a tentative promise to Balak. He said he would work for Balak and utter an oracle but that he would only speak what God instructed. Despite Balaam's clear, strong financial motivation and incentive to curse Israel, he did not do so. Instead, five times the prophet blessed the nation, obviously in defiance of his employer and seemingly against his own desire.

If there is any doubt about where Balaam's heart lay, the issue is settled by the book of Jude that says false prophets, "have rushed for profit into Balaam's error" (Jude 11). Interestingly, Jude speaks critically of Balaam, even though the prophet never actually cursed Israel; he was only willing to. We know Balaam had in his heart the desire to curse Israel, but he failed to do so. We see from the story of Balaam that men and women can be used by other people for selfish gain but can also be used by God, even despite their intentions, to accomplish His purposes.

How should we respond to the realization that we have been used by others for their gain? First, we can follow Christ's example: "When they hurled their insults at him, he did not retaliate; when he suffered, he made no threats. Instead, he entrusted himself to him who judges justly" (1 Pet. 2:23).

Second, we should respond with humility, realizing that we are capable of the same sin. As the saying goes, "But for the grace of God, go I." Paul warns us of having a "holier than thou" attitude in Romans 2:22: "You who say that people should not commit adultery, do you commit adultery? You who abhor idols, do you rob temples?" Paul's assumption is that whatever we can see in others, we probably have a little bit of it in ourselves.

Third, when recognizing we can be used by others, we should be careful. Jesus told his disciples, "I am sending you out like sheep among wolves. Therefore be as shrewd as snakes and as innocent as doves" (Matt. 10:16). There is a paradox here. To be innocent means that we drop our guard. We see no evil. We overcome our cynicism and believe the best in people. But to be as shrewd as snakes means that we are not naïve. We know what people are capable of, and we see the signs that point to danger and sin. It seems impossible to do both at the same time, but maybe instead of trying to solve the paradox, it is best to realize the trade-off. Every time we are suspicious of another person's behavior, it costs us. The cost is best counted in terms of intimacy. We all long for intimacy with the people we love. Intimacy means that you lower your guard and make yourself vulnerable. The opposite of intimacy is protection. Every time you put up your guard, it costs you intimacy; but when you lower your guard, you allow for more intimacy. Not all relationships can tolerate—nor do all relationships warrant—the same amount of vulnerability or intimacy. In our close relationships we must recognize that there is a cost to protecting ourselves (we have less intimacy), but there is also a cost to lowering our guard (we can get hurt).

Instead of asking how it is possible to be both innocent as doves and shrewd as serpents at the same time, perhaps we should ask God which of the two we are neglecting.

9

Used Emotionally

"One filled with joy preaches without preaching."
—Mother Teresa

Mother Teresa understood that joy comes from within and is not dictated by external circumstances. It is something we are filled with, and then it overflows to people around us. Not everyone operates with this understanding of joy. Some people are convinced that their emotional state is a response to the people and circumstances around them. In other words, their emotional well-being is anchored to the actions of others. They let other people use them emotionally. This is a dangerous and frustrating way to live. Not everyone allows others to have this control over them, however. I noticed as a child that my mother determined that her emotional well-being would be anchored to her actions. She refused to be used emotionally by others.

Darren: The Controller

Darren regularly approached his coworkers to express complaints or concerns. Some of these were directed at the company in general, others at the managers or workers, and some at customers. His effect on the company was exhausting, as dealing with him consumed a great deal of time. Chip, one of his coworkers, told me that he would spend an hour with Darren, and then he would spend an hour on the phone with other coworkers digesting and venting. Then Chip would often spend the rest of the day thinking about the conversation and being ineffective in his work. Chip was consumed by Darren's complaints. On several occasions Chip wasn't able to sleep at night. One of Chip's coworkers told him that he had the same reaction to the complaints, yet Darren had around him a circle of friends who were loyal to him. When I heard about this situation, I wondered how those people could be his friends. He seemed so toxic that everyone around him would quickly get burned. I wondered if he gave those friends some special treatment or pass—or if they were blind or deaf to what he was doing.

Obviously, his friends were not ignorant or untouched by his contentiousness, so it occurred to me that their ability to remain calm around him was not because they saw him differently or were treated differently by him. The difference was their attitude. Specifically, their attitude was, "I will not give Darren the ability to determine whether this is a good day or a bad day." I told Chip that I was convinced he could have the same attitude as Darren's friends who were unmoved by the incessant complaining. That attitude is more sane and peaceful, more healthy and more Christlike.

It occurs to me that I have given people like Darren more power in my life than any human should. I have given them the power to decide whether my days will be good days or bad days. My emotional well-being rises or falls on their actions. In the past, I have allowed my day to be determined by the actions of others. You probably have a few people in your life to whom you too have given that power.

The key difference between Chip and the other people who found it easier to be friends with Darren was that the others refused to give Darren emotional power. Their days were not determined by his actions. They were not emotionally used by him.

We Cannot Control Other People

Jesus spoke to His disciples about the importance of maintaining some emotional distance. He sent the twelve apostles on a missionary journey, and He instructed them to go into villages preaching and healing. He told them to pack lightly and be content with whatever provisions they had and whatever hospitality people showed them. Then Jesus told them not to put too much stock in the results. He said, "If any place will not welcome you or listen to you, shake the dust off your feet when you leave, as a testimony against them" (Mark 6:11). The shaking of dust off the feet is a warning to the observer, but it is also significant for the actor—it is an acknowledgement that the evangelist has done his job and the results are in God's hands.

This acknowledgement is vital for our own emotional health. We cannot control the behavior of other people. The point of Jesus' parable of the soils (see Matt. 13:1–9) is that when the word of God is sown, there are different responses.

The variance of responses is not the result of variation in the power of the Word of God nor in the ability of the farmer. The variation is in the heart of the person who receives it. The apostle Paul knew this, and that's why he said, "I planted the seed, Apollos watered it, but God made it grow" (1 Cor. 3:6). Paul knew that we control our actions, but that we are not able to control the response or actions of others.

James Dobson explains the importance of acknowledging our inability to control other people's beliefs and actions. This recognition is vital not only for our emotional health but for the success of our relationships. In *Love Must be Tough*, Dobson writes about a couple named Joe and Faye. Joe told his wife he no longer loved her, and Faye tried to win him back. But Dobson says Faye pushed too hard.

> Though I understand the compulsion that drives Faye to plead for Joe's attention and love, she is systematically destroying the last glimmer of hope for reconciliation. She has stripped herself of all dignity and self-respect crawling on her belly like a subservient puppy before her master. The more Joe insults her and spurns her advances, the more intensely she seems to want and need him.[1]

Faye needs to learn that her emotional well-being cannot be dependent upon the actions of another person. She must decide where her identity ends and her husband's identity begins. In her mind, there must be a boundary between these individuals. Drawing this boundary is difficult, however, especially in the midst of disaster and chaos. Dobson writes, "Panic often leads to appeasement, which is virtually never successful in seeking to control the behavior of others."[2]

I wrote a moment ago about the words Jesus gave to His disciples when He sent them on a missionary journey and how they were to shake the dust off their feet when they were rejected. On a similar journey, Jesus sent out seventy-two evangelists. When they returned, they were overjoyed that the demons had submitted to their preaching of the name of Jesus. But Jesus told them, "Do not rejoice that the spirits submit to you, but rejoice that your names are written in heaven" (Luke 10:20). We must learn to rejoice in the right things. If our happiness is dependent upon the actions of other people, we will continually be disappointed and emotionally used. But if we rejoice that our names are written in heaven, and that we can be used by God as His vessels, then we will never be disappointed.

10

(Over)used

"Learn to say 'no' and it will be of more use to you than to be able to read Latin."

—*Charles Haddon Spurgeon*

I'm not sure many of us would place much value on learning Latin (I haven't used it since college), but we can all see the value in learning the word "no." Nevertheless, it is an incredibly difficult word for most of us to utter at the right times. One of the ways we are used by others is that in our inability to say the word "no" we get overused. Often, our overuse is through doing things we enjoy, with people we love, in places we care about. We feel useful there and are delighted to be of use, but we get overused.

Byron: The Doormat

The answer to these questions became clear to me after a couple in our church ended their four-year relationship. After the breakup, the young man, Byron, became far more active in the church than ever before. But he wasn't just active, he became dependent and enmeshed in the pastors' lives. One of the pastors at our church expressed the painfully ironic admission, "I like the broken-up Byron better." This is sick. The church has a habit of using people. We send a mixed message in this way because we say that the gospel and the church serve to strengthen families. We teach on how to have strong marriages and godly children. But whom do we reward? Whom do we affirm and praise?

The church cannot voice support of family but honor those who spend less time with their families in order to support the programs of the organization. What's good for the family should be good for the church. If this is not the case, then something is wrong with the way the church is working.

It is possible that you have been overused. You know the concepts of this book all too well. Perhaps you made a decision years ago that you would be used by God, or perhaps you decided you wouldn't object to being used by others. Maybe you are the first to say yes and feel that saying no seems unloving. If that's the case, this book isn't meant to add to your pressure or to your guilt. Praise God that you have found a place and that He has found a purpose for you. Then ask God if He would have you take a break. The truly important and useful things in life have limits. Money can be overspent. Medicine can be overdosed. Clay can be overmanipulated. Wineskins can be overfilled (see Mark 2:22). You, even in your perfect niche, can be overused.

Keep in mind the fourth commandment:

> Remember the Sabbath day by keeping it holy. Six days you shall labor and do all your work, but the seventh day is a Sabbath to the LORD your God. On it you shall

not do any work, neither you, nor your son or daughter, nor your manservant or maidservant, nor your animals, nor the alien within your gates. For in six days the LORD made the heavens and the earth, the sea, and all that is in them, but he rested on the seventh day. Therefore the LORD blessed the Sabbath day and made it holy. (Exod. 20:8–11)

It is significant that this command occupies so much space within the list of Ten Commandments and that it is justified with a theological rationale. The reason we should keep the Sabbath is, in so doing, we not only obey God, but we reflect God's character. We become more godlike. It is central to God's character that He rested on the seventh day. As God's creation in His image, He has designed us to enjoy and need that same rest.

In our desire to be used, we must prevent ourselves from being overused. We are fulfilled when we are in humble, dependent service to God. This almost always involves service to others as well. But we are unfulfilled and frustrated when our primary goal is to serve anyone other than God—whether that is others or ourselves. We will find ourselves overused, and even enslaved, if we seek to serve others. But when we serve God, we find the ultimate resting place.

Perhaps you picked up this book because you saw the title *Who's Using You?* and you immediately remembered the feeling of being used by someone else. That is a repulsive, humiliating and terrible realization. Both world history and our personal histories are filled with examples of people using others. I remember listening to kids in elementary school talk about their friends who they thought were "using" them— usually to get access to their toys, food, money, outings, etc. And from childhood on we see the story repeated, but with increasing stakes and consequences and with a growing sense of betrayal. Consider the biblical story of King Xerxes, in the book of Esther, who realized he had been used.

Haman: The Opportunist

King Xerxes of ancient Persia trusted his advisor Haman too much (see Esther 3). Haman despised the Jewish people because they would not bow down to him or give him noble titles since they acknowledged only the LORD as their God and worthy of worship. The Jewish people were taken captive by Babylon, and then Babylon was conquered by Persia. Now the Jews were living as foreigners in Persia. But they didn't live like Persians, eat like them or celebrate like them. So Haman hated them.

He knew Xerxes trusted him, so he suggested a plan that would have catastrophic consequences for the Jews. He worded it generally enough that the king wouldn't realize the magnitude of what he was about to rubber-stamp. (Well, they didn't have rubber; it says he used a ring.) Haman warned the king, "There is a certain people dispersed and scattered among the peoples in all the provinces of your kingdom . . . [whose] customs are different from those of all other people, and [who] do not obey the king's laws; it is not in the king's best interest to tolerate them. If it pleases the king, let a decree be issued to destroy them" (3:8–9). The king agreed, but he didn't realize at the time that his own wife was a Jewess who was included among the group he had just doomed to annihilation. When that revelation finally came, Xerxes realized he had been used.

Being used isn't always bad. If we discover we are used by God, we rejoice. If we find we are used by our friends who we trust, we are glad to be of service. But the thought of being used by others for harm—especially unknowingly and unwillingly—is deeply painful. There is something liberating, however, about realizing we have been used by others. It's our moment of truth that helps us make sense of what's going on and why things are not right. It's our wake-up call that makes tomorrow a new day as we determine we will no longer be used by others and instead will be vessels exclusively for God's use.

PART THREE

Used by the Enemy

PART THREE

11

(Conf)used

"We live in an age disturbed, confused, bewildered, afraid of its own forces, in search not merely of its road but even of its direction."
—*President Woodrow Wilson*

Sometimes we are used by God as an instrument of correction. But sometimes we take this too far, and we become confused. Some people think they are used by God more than they actually are. These self-appointed prophets had the defining moment of transformation described in this book when they prayed a prayer of availability to God. They want to be used by God as vessels of truth. Though well-intentioned, the lines are blurred for them between what God wants and what they want, between what God thinks and what they think. They see themselves being used by God in every situation to right what is wrong, to correct what is false and to administer wisdom wherever they see folly. They have become confused about their role and their authority.

Scott: The Plumb Line

Scott, for instance, was always convinced that what he saw as good was also right. He thought his company should be selling fewer products—just the high markup ones so they could still have a high profit. He crusaded for this idea with his boss, the accountant and all his coworkers. After several conversations, his boss made it clear that he wasn't convinced. The accountant was also not sure that the suggestion made sense. But Scott wouldn't give up. His daily mission was to convince those around him of his idea, even after it had received a fair hearing and was rejected. It became an ethical issue for him. In his mind, for the company not to implement his idea was morally wrong. Scott was confused about his role in the company, and he was confused about the difference between "good" and "right."

The ancient Greek philosophers Socrates, Plato and Aristotle were preoccupied with defining the good and the right. Interestingly, they knew there was a difference between the two. Often today, we confuse the two and think that whatever we deem good must also be right. Right is a moral quality of absolute nature. But good is a comparative quality and is often subjective. This means that while the Bible is able to speak authoritatively to you and me about what is morally right, the Bible does not necessarily illumine for us what is a wise, good or prudent course of action for us to take in every situation. When it comes to correcting someone, we should focus on what is morally right or wrong and let the authority of the Bible speak for itself. We cross the line when the issue is about making a good choice or deciding between what you think is wise and what I think is wise. In these cases, we can offer our advice (preferably when solicited) but not our correction.

The Bible addresses many situations where we must give people the freedom of conscience to decide what is right and wrong for themselves. Paul illustrated this with his discussion of eating meat sacrificed to idols.

> If some unbeliever invites you to a meal and you want to go, eat whatever is put before you without raising questions of conscience. But if anyone says to you, "This has been offered in sacrifice," then do not eat it, both for the sake of the man who told you and for conscience' sake— the other man's conscience, I mean, not yours. For why should my freedom be judged by another's conscience? (1 Cor. 10:27–29)

Paul was not giving a specific command in Scripture whether or not to eat meat sacrificed to idols. His command was to let other people make up their own minds and to support their decision by honoring their wishes when with them. This is, of course, not true of biblical commands. But in areas where the Bible is silent, we have freedom to do what the Holy Spirit guides us to do and what we think is best.

(Conf)used about Control

In many cases, it is clear that a loved one has not only acted unwisely but also wrongly. In these cases we can offer our correction, but we still cannot control the other person's behavior or response. Our job, therefore, is to speak the truth in love (see Eph. 4:15), without regard to the other person's likelihood to change or our ability to control his or her behavior.

Think of the many ways we would like to control the behavior of other people but cannot:

- Your child lies to you.
- Your child bullies his friends when you are not around.

- Your wife carelessly wastes money.
- Your husband looks at pornography.
- The person you share your faith with won't convert.
- Your adult father won't stop being rude to you.
- Your adult son says he's gay.

In each of these cases, we have sufficient biblical ground to confront the person we love. We have every right to expect a change in their behavior and even to ask for it. But we become confused when we assume that we are able to control the other person's response. If you think you can control someone else's behavior, you are confused about your role in the universe. The Bible reminds us of our place: "God is in heaven and you are on earth, so let your words be few" (Eccles. 5:2). Your role is not to control other people but to speak the truth to them. God is the one in control.

Merely speaking the truth to someone may seem ridiculously insufficient. You sense that every time you say something it goes in one ear and out the other. However, if you speak to someone and the word goes in one ear and out the other, you need to recognize that you did not speak the word of God. God's word doesn't do that. Isaiah tells us, "My word that goes out from my mouth: It will not return to me empty, but will accomplish what I desire and achieve the purpose for which I sent it" (Isa. 55:11).

As a vessel for God's use, when you speak the truth to someone, you are only supplemental to God's work. God has already been at work in the other person's life. When you speak the truth to them, you merely augment the ongoing work God is doing in shaping their heart. After you finish speaking, the word of God continues to penetrate deep into their heart and soul. To avoid getting confused, we must remember that we are supplements to the work of God, not central to it. It is our responsibility to be available vessels, not to enforce change.

The Sovereignty of God

The *Westminster Shorter Catechism* asks, "What is the chief end of man?" And the answer in the confession is, "Man's chief end is to glorify God, and to enjoy him for ever."[1] John Piper often summarizes the idea in this way: "God is most glorified in us when we are most satisfied in him."[2]

To be used by God is an affirmation of your belief in God's sovereignty (that God is in control of everything in the universe). God is pleased and glorified when you are satisfied that He is doing a good job of being in control of the world. But sometimes we get confused rather than used. We believe that God is not doing a sufficient job at being in control. He is silent or passive, and we feel we need to step in.

To some extent, it needs to be okay that things don't always go as we wish. Not only will excessive dissatisfaction drive us crazy, it is an offense to God. It says that God is not living up to His job description as the Sovereign One. I say it needs to be okay "to some extent" because we are not called to apathy or laziness. Realization that the world is not all as it should be ought to drive us to action, but it needs to be a dependent action. It should not drive us to the independent action of "making ourselves useful" but instead to the dependent action of being used by God.

12

Use(rs)

"Drunkenness is temporary suicide; the happiness that it brings is merely negative, a momentary cessation of unhappiness."

—*John Ruskin*

D rugs want to use you. But they don't have feelings or plans, so they can't really "use" anything. Drug sellers, however, can use you. And other drug users want to use you to justify and legitimate their own habit. Of course, it's better to acknowledge that the devil wants to destroy you by getting you to use drugs.

James: The Counterculturist

James had a dramatic conversion to Christianity and became passionate about living in obedience to God. In many ways he became radical in his faith and was willing to live extremely counterculturally. He and his wife gave up going to the movies, bought only organic and unprocessed food, and homeschooled their children.

As a part of their new countercultural life, James gave up smoking pot. He had gone several years without buying, selling or smoking pot by the time I met him. But he confided something to me that was very revealing. For the last several years, he had kept one marijuana plant in his closet. He didn't add "just in case" to the admission, because I don't think that was the point. It wasn't just in case he had a sudden urge for a joint. He is a man of great self-control, so that wasn't why the lonely plant sat in the dark—literally "in the closet." He kept the plant in the closet because he was not sure he wanted to completely die to his old self.

The apostle Paul said, "We know that our old self was crucified with him in order that the body of sin might be brought to nothing, so that we would no longer be enslaved to sin" (Rom. 6:6 ESV). James still wanted a part of his old self. He had not had the transforming moment that is the central theme of this book. He knew that he had not genuinely had a change of identity. He had not authentically said about drugs, "This is not who I am." He stopped smoking pot, but he had not made the heartfelt declaration: "I will not be used by Satan in this way. I am not a drug user." So while he was able to practice an outward discipline that exceeds most people, he knew those changes lacked the right foundation.

As you can imagine, even though he went several years drug free, it didn't last forever. Eventually he started smoking again. And it wasn't because one day he was overcome with temptation and fell off the wagon. It was because he wanted to go back to his old self. He decided to start living consistently as a person who is willing to use drugs and be used by them. The story ends well, though. A few years later he recognized the price he was paying and the toll it was taking on his family, and the genuine transformational moment came. It was only through the declaration of a new identity—"I am not a pot user"—that he was able to make a lasting change.

I discovered another user while on Facebook. Keeping up on Facebook is a part of my job; and, while I was tending to my flock and my "wall," I noticed that Blake, one of our young adults, had joined a group to legalize marijuana. I looked further into his profile and discovered that this is a big passion for him. He has the tie-dyed clothes, hair and lingo that one may expect for a crusader of this cause. We discussed this issue; and he conceded that since the Bible says we should obey the governing authorities, as long as marijuana is illegal, a Christian should abstain. But he was adamant that once legalized, there would be no moral/biblical reason for prohibiting smoking pot.

This is where the concept of being used by God is valuable. Paul wrote, "Do not get drunk on wine, which leads to debauchery. Instead, be filled with the Spirit" (Eph. 5:18). I asked Blake how available he is to be used by God when he is high on marijuana. We are vessels with finite capacity. Like a glass, if we are filled with water, we have no room for anything else. To make room for some oil, some water must be displaced. So if a Christian's mind and spirit is partially filled with wine (or any other drug), his capacity to be filled with the Holy Spirit is diminished by that degree.

The question, then, is not whether marijuana is okay to smoke if it becomes legal but how much you want to be used by the Holy Spirit. If you want to be completely available for God to use you, then you will make room for Him. If you want to be completely under the influence of the Holy Spirit, you will not allow yourself to be under the influence of anything else. Don't expect God to share the vessel. Moses warned, "Do not worship any other god, for the LORD, whose name is Jealous, is a jealous God" (Exod. 34:14). In other words, God doesn't share His temple, His glory or His vessels.

13

Used to Slander

"It takes your enemy and your friend, working together, to hurt you to the heart; the one to slander you and the other to get the news to you."

—Mark Twain

One way the devil uses each of us is to spread gossip or slander. Gossip is one of those words that is almost impossible to define. Most people define the word as "talking behind someone's back," but we talk about other people all the time and there's no harm. Sometimes we are even trying to help. Like so many other sins, the best way to define it is to discern the motive. Gossip is "speaking about someone behind their back, in any way not motivated by love." None of us is immune to being used in this way.

Gary: The Advocate

For a few years during seminary, I was the pastor of a rural church in Indiana. I was fortunate to have a loyal friend named Gary who served with me as the youth pastor. One summer afternoon, when I had become particularly discouraged with the church politics and divisive factions, I unloaded my frustrations to him. Please understand, these were not prayer requests. What I engaged in was an hour of slander and gossip, denouncing every person who made my life difficult. Gary listened graciously for a while; but when I wore myself down and came to a break, Gary shook his head a little and I could tell something profound was about to emerge. I had hoped he would be profoundly sympathetic to my tirade. But instead, he said, "Dan, do you have any idea how much Jesus loves His bride?"

That's when I had a transformational moment. For an hour I had been used by Satan to slander Jesus' best friend. The church is called a lot of things in the Bible: the body of Christ, the household of God, the heavenly Jerusalem. But the climactic image of the church in Revelation is the bride of Christ, beautifully adorned and ready for a great wedding feast. Consider the things said about this bride. She is pure, blameless, robed in white. The apostle Paul said of her, "I promised you to one husband, to Christ, so that I might present you as a pure virgin to him" (2 Cor. 11:2). Jesus not only loves her, He actually likes her and thinks highly of her! Yet I had been used to put her down. The church is the precious bride of Christ, and each member of it has a special place prepared at the great wedding feast. I cannot expect to please Christ while talking disrespectfully of His bride.

Paul admonishes, "Do not let any unwholesome talk come out of your mouths, but only what is helpful for building others up according to their needs, that it may benefit those who listen" (Eph. 4:29).

One way to avoid being used as a tool for slander is to recognize that we never have the whole story. My identical twin brother and I both happened to have babies born in the same hospital within a six-week period of each other. My daughter, Rebekah, was born at St. Joseph's in mid-March. Ken's daughter, Kate, was born at the end of May, with the same nurse attending his wife who had helped mine. I remembered the nurse when I came into the hospital room to visit my newborn niece because she had taken an interest in our family six weeks prior, and we seemed to have a good rapport with her. But I did not realize how much turmoil this nurse was feeling while my identical twin brother was by a different woman's side. When I came to visit my niece, as soon as I walked in the room, the nurse burst out with a loud sigh of relief. One could tell that she had been in private anguish for some time, wondering whether or not to tell this new mother that her partner had borne a daughter to another woman just a few weeks earlier! I can just imagine her on break with other nurses, debating when, how or if to break the news to this unfortunate patient.

With such simple mix-ups, it's easy to see why Jesus said, "Judge not, that you be not judged" (Matt. 7:1, ESV). We may not always have such a quick, easy or clear explanation of why other people behave the way they do. Our best bet is to determine that we will be used by God as a tool of encouragement and to avoid the devil's desire to use us as a tool of slander. Each of us has a choice: we will either be used by the devil to slander the bride of Christ or be used by God to build her up.

14

Used to Tempt

*"Anybody can be good in the country.
There are no temptations there."*
—Oscar Wilde

Short of leaving this planet, we have no way to escape temptation. And even in some other universe, we'd still be accompanied by our own mind and soul and have plenty of sin to dream up. One consistent teaching in the Bible about temptation is that the object itself is not the problem. The devil tempts people, people tempt people, and people entertain their own temptations, but the objects themselves are never blamed. Even the most godly people in the Bible recognized that they had been used by the devil to tempt, as we'll see below.

Peter: The Voice

Jesus knew the cross was in His future. During His last few days in the garden of Gethsemane, He prayed that God would prevent Him from suffering crucifixion, if there were any other way. But then He affirmed, "Not my will, but yours be done" (Luke 22:42). Despite His resolution to do what was necessary (die on the cross), He faced difficulty in submitting to that fate in the garden of Gethsemane, and that wasn't His only obstacle. Earlier in His ministry, Jesus told the disciples what lay ahead, and Peter would have nothing of it. He said "Never, Lord. . . . This shall never happen to you" (Matt. 16:22).

At this point one could ask, "Where did Peter get that idea from?" There are a few possibilities. Perhaps the idea of keeping Christ from the cross stemmed from his own imagination. It could be that the instinct of protecting others was ingrained in his family and he'd seen it modeled by his parents. Then again, maybe this was a thought the devil fed to Peter; maybe the idea had its origin outside of Peter's mind. This is what Jesus perceived. Jesus said to Peter, "Out of my sight, Satan! You are a stumbling block to me; you do not have in mind the things of God, but the things of men" (16:23). Jesus was not angry at Peter. This was not His way of exhibiting how frustrated He was with Peter by sounding extreme. Nor was Jesus calling Peter names. He wasn't comparing Peter to Satan or saying Peter was acting like the devil. Jesus was talking to Satan, not Peter. And by so doing, He illustrated that Peter had been used by Satan to tempt Jesus. This is not a criticism of Peter, and doesn't make him worse than you or me. It just means that men and women are vessels that can be used by God, by each other or by the devil.

Maybe you're still hesitant to see Peter, or anyone else, as being used by the devil. Maybe it sounds too harsh to accept. But consider the alternative; Jesus could have said to Peter,

"That's a really stupid idea." Or he could have said, "Peter, you are coming up with evil ideas, you must be evil yourself." But instead, Jesus recognized that Peter was neither the problem nor the enemy. Recognizing that we can be used as instruments of the devil is a gracious way of dealing with our friends, family and enemies. It reminds us that no human being is truly our enemy. Ephesians 6:12 says, "For our struggle is not against flesh and blood, but against the rulers, against the authorities, against the powers of this dark world and against the spiritual forces of evil in the heavenly realms."

My struggle is not with you, with my wife, with my kids, with difficult church members or even with any human enemy. My struggle is with the spiritual forces of evil. I understand that I can be used by Satan to tempt others to sin and that they can be used in the same way. Once I remind myself of this truth, I see the people around me as co-strugglers, not as enemies.

Interestingly, though secular psychologists are unlikely to agree that the devil seeks to ruin relationships, many do agree with the wisdom of changing our mind about who is the enemy. Psychologist Michael White calls this process "externalizing conversations." His goal is to help clients see that their problems are not purely internal or even purely relational. Instead, he says a problem exists that is outside of the relationship. In White's *Maps of Narrative Practice*, he writes:

> "Many people who seek therapy believe that the problems in their lives are a reflection of their own identity or the identity of others. When this is the case, their efforts to resolve problems usually have the effect of exacerbating them instead. This leads people to even more solidly believe that the problems of their lives are a reflection

of certain 'truths' about their nature and their character or about the nature and character of others—that these problems are internal to their self or the selves of others."[1]

White offers an example of a child with ADHD who believes that his problem is within himself. His parents believe the problem is in their child. As long as they approach the problem of ADHD in this way, the child is the enemy. But White encourages the parents to view ADHD as the problem. He envisions ADHD as an entity of its own. It has desires. It has plans and schemes. It wants to destroy the relationship between child and parents.

Obviously, ADHD is not a person and does not have thoughts, desires or plans. But White's therapeutic approach involves envisioning it as such in order to remind the family that they are all on the same side.

White's explanation of externalizing conversations helps illustrate why being mindful of the devil's schemes is helpful for relationships. If we can speak of ADHD as having a life of its own where it uses people for its own desires and plans, how much more can we speak of the devil using us?

As Christians, we trust the Bible when it tells us the devil really does have thoughts, desires and plans (and these terms aren't a metaphor like they were with the example of ADHD). By being mindful of the devil's schemes, we can make ourselves more available to be used by God—as opposed to being used by Satan. In fact, that mindfulness shows biblical wisdom. Paul tells the Corinthians that he would not harbor unforgiveness, "in order that Satan might not outwit us. For we are not unaware of his schemes" (2 Cor. 2:11).

When we sin, we make a statement about what we believe regarding God, the world and others. These statements are always based on lies, served up and delivered by Satan. The serpent's method of using human beings has always been the same.

Adam: The Pawn

Adam and Eve were used. They were in the garden of Eden, and God commanded them not to eat of the fruit of the Tree of the Knowledge of Good and Evil. We read the following regarding the serpent's temptation in Genesis:

> He [the serpent] said to the woman, "Did God really say, 'You must not eat from any tree in the garden'?"
>
> The woman said to the serpent, "We may eat fruit from the trees in the garden, but God did say, 'You must not eat fruit from the tree that is in the middle of the garden, and you must not touch it, or you will die.'"
>
> "You will not surely die," the serpent said to the woman. "For God knows that when you eat of it your eyes will be opened, and you will be like God, knowing good and evil." (Gen. 3:1–5)

Both Adam and Eve ate of the fruit. Most people immediately recognize that the man and woman were used by Satan to join his rebellion against God. Satan's method of deception is subtler; rather than sheer temptation to sin, he also made it seem as if the fruit were enticing in and of itself. The serpent put doubt in Eve's mind by asking, "Did God really say . . . ?" The deception was effective, for Eve's account does not match up with what we previously read. She tells the serpent that she was not to touch the tree, but God's original command was only that she not eat the fruit. The temptation ends with a lie, but the most effective lies always have a kernel of truth in them. Satan said that she would become like God (not true), knowing good and evil (true).

The sin of desiring to be like God has a notorious legacy in Scripture. It is no surprise, therefore, that throughout Scripture pride is often seen as the worst of all sins, and the attitude from which all other sins derive. The King of Babylon also desired to become like God, and this was his downfall. We read, "You said in your heart, 'I will ascend to heaven; I will raise my throne above the stars of God; I will sit enthroned on the mount of assembly, on the utmost heights of the sacred mountain. I will ascend above the tops of the clouds; I will make myself like the Most High'" (Isa. 14:13–14). .

We know that Adam and Eve were used by Satan. But it's important to see how this occurred as this is the first sin related in the Bible and as it expresses an enduring method of Satan. Whenever human beings sin, they first believe a lie. Sin is always a statement of faith. When Adam ate the fruit, he made a statement about what he believed. He essentially said one or all of the following:

- "God didn't really mean what he said."
- "It's not that bad."
- "God doesn't know what's best for me."
- "God doesn't want what's best for me."
- "I will be happier if I eat this fruit."

All of these are statements of faith about God and the world, and all of them are lies. Every sin is like this. Consider the person tempted to commit adultery. That act is a statement of faith. The same lies are uttered:

- "God didn't really mean what he said."

- "It's not that bad."
- "God doesn't know what's best for me."
- "God doesn't want what's best for me."
- "I will be happier if I [sin]."

As a vessel for God's use, we need to remember that the devil's desire is to detract us from that task. There is a moment of transformation when we realize that we can be used by God. Likewise, there is a moment of transformation when we realize we can be used by the devil. For some, this is a shocking realization that they do not operate independently within the world with all their own ideas and always acting of their own free will.

Dave: The Lie Detector

Dave's life changed in a moment when he recognized that he had been used by the devil. He is a husband and father who developed an addiction to pornography, drank excessively at parties and occasionally used drugs. He grew up in the church; but as he got older, Christ was no longer the center of his life. Eventually, his faith was a faint memory of the past. But the drugs, alcohol and pornography were not satisfying him, so he became depressed. He began counseling with a psychologist who prescribed him antidepressants. The drugs seemed to have no effect; so he asked the counselor whether he ought to turn to God, given that nothing else was working. The psychologist said, "God cannot do anything for your depression."

After hearing this pronouncement from the psychologist, Dave immediately went home and dumped his antidepressants in the trash. Dave told this story to a men's group at our church; and when he got to this point of the narrative, one of the men in the group observed, "Satan overplayed his card!" Dave hadn't given God much thought, but he knew that he had encountered a blasphemous lie. Had the doctor simply said, "I don't think it will help much," perhaps Dave would have agreed and dropped the idea of coming back to the Lord. But Dave knew where the phrase "God can't do anything for you" came from. At that point, Satan made it all too obvious to Dave that he was in the midst of a spiritual battle for his soul.

Jesus said, "The thief comes only to steal and kill and destroy; I have come that they may have life, and have it to the full" (John 10:10). Up until the moment the doctor told Dave not to turn to God, he was unaware that the devil's plan was to steal, kill and destroy. That unawareness gave him the impression that either his struggles were his own or the people around him were responsible for making his life miserable. But when he came face-to-face with the words of Satan, he was liberated and encouraged with the realization that human beings were not his primary enemy. He was also alarmed that he had bought into satanic lies without knowing it and that he had been used unwittingly in a demonic scheme to steal, kill and destroy his own family and soul.

Dave's life changed the moment he realized that he had been used. Your life can change as well when you determine no longer to be used by the enemy, but to be used by God.

15

Used to Promote Legalism

"I am astonished that you are so quickly deserting him who called you in the grace of Christ and are turning to a different gospel."

Galatians 1:6, ESV

Godly obedience is *keeping* the commands of the Bible. Legalism is *adding to* the commands of the Bible. The apostle Paul addressed legalism in the book of Romans. The church had made up several laws in addition to the biblical ones. These laws included the observance of certain holidays and the prohibition of eating meat sacrificed to idols. Paul encouraged the church to "accept him whose faith is weak, without passing judgment on disputable matters" (14:1). Paul determined that in matters that were not explicitly addressed in Scripture, it was better to live at peace with one another. He admonished, "So whatever you believe about these things keep between yourself and God" (14:22).

Mark: The Lawgiver

Once I attended church with a friend who belonged to a different denomination; and her youth leader, Mark, told me that I was not allowed to take communion. To do so, he said, would be inappropriate since Methodists and Lutherans have a different view of the Lord's Supper. Even then, it struck me as ironic that the feast called "communion" could be so divisive. The youth leader's prohibition seemed legalistic to me. But that experience was the first of many my friend and I encountered in the church that would divide relationships.

These divisions are often caused by legalism. For instance, a woman in our church had a C-section after difficulty in childbirth, but she refused to let anyone know; so her husband helped keep the secret. In the end, some parishioners got a sense that a big secret about the birth was being contained; and when word got around, this young woman felt terribly shamed. Her shame was the result of a conference she had attended where the teacher had said that it was unbiblical to have a caesarean. She felt inadequate and ungodly. She was the victim of legalism, and she experienced the unnecessary pain accompanied by it.

There are countless ways that the church promotes legalism, despite repeated biblical injunctions against these "extra laws." Contemporary legalistic causes include: prohibition of music with drumbeats, absolute insistence on homeschooling, unwavering prohibition of women working, etc. Supporters of legalism create two classes of believers—regular Christians and "super-Christians." Elitism is the result. In addition, the guilt of those in the "lesser" class is often unnecessary as they have not violated a biblical command.

In *The Grace Awakening*, Charles Swindoll explains how willing Christians are to allow, endorse or promote legalism.

> We'll go to the wall and square off against any enemy who threatens to take away our national freedom, but we'll not be nearly so passionate as Christians under grace to fight for our rightful liberty. Let enough legalists come aboard and we will virtually give them command of the ship. We will fear their frowns, we will adapt our lives to their lists, we'll allow ourselves to be intimidated, and for the sake of peace at any price we will succumb to their agenda.[1]

It is a mystery why we so quickly forsake the freedom that we have in Christ and allow ourselves to be used by legalists. We can be used by others to promote their legalistic causes; in so doing, we support the division between Christians and people who imagine themselves to be "super-Christians." We can be used by Satan to promote legalism; in so doing, we create division in the church and cast unnecessary guilt on others. But we can also be used by God to reject legalism and be vessels of unity and peace in the church.

PART FOUR

Used by God

16

(Enth)used

"Enthusiast: one who vainly imagines a private revelation; one who has a vain confidence of his intercourse with God"

—*Samuel Johnson's Dictionary*

Samuel Johnson is 99 percent right in his definition of enthusiast. The word "enthused" comes from two Greek words: *en*, meaning "filled," and *theos*, meaning "god." So to be enthused literally means "to be filled with God." The point of contention, of course, is whether it is vain or incorrect to believe one has heard from God. If you want to be used by God, you must first be enthused by the Holy Spirit.

Pentecost: The Day of Filling

We read in Acts, "When the day of Pentecost came, they were all together in one place. Suddenly a sound like the blowing of a violent wind came from heaven and filled the whole house where they were sitting. They saw what seemed to be tongues of fire that separated and came to rest on each of them. All of them were filled with the Holy Spirit and began to speak in other tongues as the Spirit enabled them" (Acts 2:1–4). On this incredible day, Christians were filled with the Holy Spirit, and the result was obvious to others. These enthused disciples were accused of drunkenness because they were speaking in tongues, but Peter argued that they couldn't be drunk since it was still morning! On the contrary, Peter explained that this occurrence was prophesied by the prophet Joel hundreds of years earlier—that in the last days God's people would experience miraculous signs.

That day of Pentecost, though unique in many ways, is also normative in the sense that all believers in Christ are filled with the Holy Spirit. The Bible tells us that the following people were filled with the Spirit:

- Bezalel was filled with the Spirit to skillfully adorn Moses' tabernacle.
- Joshua was filled with the Spirit to lead the Israelites into the Promised Land.
- Micah was filled with the Spirit to speak to Israel about the nation's sin.
- John the Baptist was filled with the Spirit from birth.
- John the Baptist's mother, Elizabeth, and father, Zechariah, were both filled with the Spirit to prophesy.
- Peter was filled with the Spirit to speak boldly—even in the face of imprisonment and unbelief.
- Paul was filled with the Spirit to speak boldly, prophesy and work miracles.

The same Holy Spirit who enthused the people above also lives among us. Jesus explained and expected that "anyone who has faith in me will do what I have been doing. He will do even greater things than these, because I am going to the Father" (John 14:12). In other words, we can be used by the Holy Spirit to speak and heal. Actually, we not only *can*; we are *commanded* to "be filled with the Spirit" (Eph. 5:18). This is not something we have to make happen; instead it is a consequence of surrendering our lives to the lordship of Christ. By "lordship," I mean that we allow Jesus to be the king of every aspect of our life. We give Him control over our desires, beliefs and actions. Paul explains, "Do you not know that your body is a temple of the Holy Spirit, who is in you, whom you have received from God?" (1 Cor. 6:19). Every believer has the Holy Spirit living within and is enthused. We can all be used by the Holy Spirit.

Renowned evangelist Billy Graham knows that each day is an opportunity to be used by God as we are filled with the Holy Spirit.

> I find it helpful to begin each day by silently committing that day into God's hands. . . . And then I step out in faith, knowing that His Holy Spirit is filling me continually as I trust in Him and obey His word. Sometimes during the day I may not be aware of His presence; sometimes I am. But at the end of the day, I can look back and thank him, because I see His hand at work. He promised to be with me that day—and He has been![1]

Bottom line? To be completely used by God, we have to be completely filled. My wife and her father operate a moon bounce (jumping castle) business, and they have received some interesting calls from customers over the years. One woman called in a panic during her party saying, "There's something wrong with this bounce house. I need you to bring another one right away. It blows up, but as soon as I turn it off it deflates again. It won't stay up." She was envisioning something more of a balloon than a bounce house, which only works when the motor is running. Similarly, we are meant to be continually filled with the Holy Spirit. The apostle Paul wrote, "And do not get drunk with wine, for that is debauchery, but be filled with the Spirit" (Eph. 5:18, ESV). If you want to be used by God, make yourself available to be filled with the Spirit. The degree to which we can be used by God depends completely on the degree to which we are enthused by the Holy Spirit.

Being used by God is a conscious choice. It does not come naturally or accidentally. We must recognize we have been used by others or by the devil and determine that from now on, God will use us, no matter the cost. Consider the story of Esther who made this conscious decision, even though it could have cost her her life.

Esther: The Reluctant Queen

A long time ago in ancient Persia, a royal advisor named Haman tricked the Persian King Xerxes into issuing an order for the extermination of all Jews in the realm. Xerxes' wife, a Jewish woman who came under the king's death order, was named Esther. She was also used but in a very different way. Esther knew that the Jews were about to be destroyed, but she understandably reasoned that she couldn't do anything about it, so she resolved to do nothing. But her cousin Mordecai visited her and explained, "If you remain silent at this time, relief and deliverance for the Jews will arise from another place, but you and your father's family will perish. And who knows but that you have come to royal position for such a time as this?" (Esther 4:14). Mordecai knew that human beings are not independent agents to the extent that we imagine. We do not simply serve ourselves when we act;

our actions serve the agendas of others. If Esther failed to act, God would find someone else.

But God had orchestrated the circumstances so that Esther would be in the perfect position to be used for the deliverance of the Jews. Esther realized the profundity of her unique situation, and though her first inclination was to do nothing, she was convinced by Mordecai of the incredible opportunity she had to be used by God. She was faced with a defining moment about who she would be. Already her identity had changed significantly. She was an insignificant Jewish foreigner who perchance became the wife of a powerful king. She could have contented herself with this identity alone, but she chose to be used by God. She mustered these incredible, timeless words of courage, "I will go to the king, even though it is against the law. And if I perish, I perish" (Esther 4:16).

The courage and plan was worth the risk. King Xerxes discovered how he had been used by Haman, and he hanged the deceiver. The Jews were spared, and Esther has long been remembered as a woman who was used by God to deliver the Jews in their long history of attempted annihilation.

17

(Transf)used

"Therefore, if anyone is in Christ, he is a new creation. The old has passed away; behold, the new has come."

2 Corinthians 5:17, ESV

The reason people lack purpose and meaning in life is that they have not been transfused. They still have their old life, their old nature and their old desires. They still insist on being used by others and by the devil. Their intention to be used is still essentially self-centered.

Saul: The Hater

In the New Testament we read of Saul of Tarsus. He was strong, stubborn and high achieving. He sings his own praises: "If anyone else thinks he has reasons to put confidence in the flesh, I have more: circumcised on the eighth day, of the people of Israel, of the tribe of Benjamin, a Hebrew of Hebrews; in regard to the law, a Pharisee; as for zeal, persecuting the church; as for legalistic righteousness, faultless."

(Phil. 3:4–6). No doubt Paul saw himself as an independent agent, used by no one. But on the road to Damascus he met the resurrected Jesus, and he came to grips with the fact that he had been used by the devil to persecute the church of God.

That was the first half of Saul's life—the half where he was used by the Enemy. But Christ changed Saul's name to Paul. Paul repented of his persecution, self-righteousness and rejection of Jesus. After his conversion, he found new purpose in life.

That said, Paul missed out on being one of the original apostles. He did not follow Jesus during the Lord's earthly ministry. Twelve other men fulfilled that role (though Judas later betrayed Jesus and was replaced by Matthias). Paul could have wallowed in self-pity and lamented that his opportunity to be used by God for something great had passed. But Paul found a unique way to be used by God, since his own situation was also unique. The other twelve apostles ministered solely to the Jews. Paul found a new, larger audience. He wrote, "For God, who was at work in the ministry of Peter as an apostle to the Jews, was also at work in my ministry as an apostle to the Gentiles" (Gal. 2:8). Paul would be used to bring the gospel to a new group of people who had not yet heard the good news. He was a missionary to the Gentiles.

Paul's story is one of the many great biblical accounts of God's second chances. His transformation from being used by the Enemy of Christianity to being radically used by God illustrates that it is never too late for any of us. But this is not simply a story of being reused; it is one of being transfused. Paul's change was not the result of sheer willpower. He did not convert from being an agent of evil to an agent of healing simply because he tried harder. His is not an example merely of self-improvement—nor is that the case with any Christian who finds purpose and is used by God. The difference between the former and latter life is not one of incremental improvement. It is one of re-creation. Paul found his latter life useful to God because his former self had died and a new self had come to life. He writes, "Therefore, if anyone is in Christ, he is a new creation. The old has passed away; behold, the new has come." (2 Cor. 5:17, ESV). Jesus first made this truth clear to Nicodemus, to whom he said, "You must be born again" (John 3:7).

We find our usefulness to God not when we try harder, but when we are transfused with new life—when we die to our former ambitions, desires, and self-worship and come to the new life of worship to God.

John Piper: Used to Give God Glory

In *Don't Waste Your Life*, John Piper explains how God has designed each of us to find purpose and meaning in being used by Him. Piper tells the story of a man who realized late in life that he had been used for worthless purposes. Piper writes, "God opened his heart to the Gospel of Christ, and he was saved from his sins and given eternal life. But that did not stop him from sobbing and saying, as the tears ran down his wrinkled face . . . 'I've wasted it! I've wasted it!'"[1]

Piper warns us about our purpose: "The answer, my friend, is not yours to invent or create. It will be decided for you. It is outside you. It is real and objective and firm. One day you will hear it. You don't create it. You don't' define it. It comes to you, and sooner or later you conform to it—or bow to it."[2]

So what is our primary purpose in life? Piper answers for himself and invites others to share in his discovery: "If my life was to have a single, all-satisfying , unifying passion, it would have to be God's passion . . . God's passion [is] the display of his own glory and the delight of my heart."[3]

Piper quotes Jonathan Edwards who also found the satisfaction and joy of being used by God: "Resolved, never to lose one moment of time; but improve it the most profitable way I possibly can."[4] Edward's determination to make every day useful for God was shared by Paul, who wrote, "Be very careful, then, how you live—not as unwise but as wise, making the most of every opportunity, because the days are evil" (Eph. 5:15–16).

Isn't Being Used a Bad Thing?

We know from the Bible that God's purpose in making people was to give Himself glory. We read in Isaiah 43:6–7:

> "Bring my sons from afar
> and my daughters from the ends of the earth—
> everyone who is called by my name,
> whom I created for my glory,
> whom I formed and made."

This is a shocking and disappointing discovery for many Christians. They recognize that they have been wrongly used by others and by the devil. Being used by others has caused them great pain, so they conclude that for someone to use another is always selfish and therefore always wrong. But then they hear that God also uses people. John Piper explains, "For many people this is not obviously an act of love. They do not feel loved when they are told that God created them for his glory. They feel used."[5]

But could it be that it is not always wrong for someone to use another? What if being used by another was in your best interest and ended up serving you better than if you had not been used in that way? Wouldn't that be the ultimate win-win situation? We say yes, but we are still skeptical. My wife would be justifiably suspicious if I said to her, "It is in your best interest to give me glory." Her suspicion is based on a true observation that in the past I have not always had her best interest in mind. I have failed to put her first. But God does not fail. His love is flawless and enduring. There is nothing wrong in being used by Him, so there is nothing inherently wrong in being used.

That said, it is wrong to use someone selfishly. And since we humans have such a strong propensity for selfishness, we are right to be suspicious of being used by anyone else. Since God's track record is better, we stand to gain much by being used by Him.

John Piper compares the relationship God has with us to a father with his child. Though humans are fallible, we get brief glimpses of times when we are rightly used by others. Piper writes, "No child complains, 'I am being used' when his father delights to make the child happy with his own presence."[6] Every once in a while we get it right; we experience being used by another person to give him or her pleasure, and in so doing, we are served as well.

Not only is God allowed to use people for His glory, it would actually be quite cruel for Him to deny us that joy. That's because we and the universe were designed for this purpose. Piper explains, "To make [people] feel good about themselves when they are made to feel good about seeing God is like taking someone to the Alps and locking them in a room full of mirrors."[7]

If you hesitate to accept the idea that it is okay for God to use people, consider the options. If God were not using you, someone else would be. And even if you succeeded in being used only by yourself, you would always be looking at a mirror rather than experiencing the greatness of God. Piper encourages, "Suppose you answer, 'I want to enjoy making much of God, not me . . .' If you respond this way, then you will have an answer to the fear that you are just being used by God when he creates you for his glory."[8]

As a Christian, you have been transfused with new life. That is the only reason your vessel is of use to the Potter.

18

(Exc)used

"No doubt Jack the Ripper excused himself on the grounds that it was human nature."

—A.A. Milne

Everyone used by God has also been excused by God. We have all sinned, yet we have all been forgiven. Some people argue that such forgiveness is unjust, too cheap, too easy, too good to be true—yet that is the promise of the gospel. The honor to be used by God is preceded by the grace of being excused.

In our culture, some people get excused of their crimes undeservedly or prematurely. This can happen because of laziness, intentional injustice, bureaucratic loopholes or just plain ignorance. Others are excused because of grace, compassion or exoneration. When the guilty are excused, we are indignant. When the innocent are excused after much turmoil, we are elated. It raises the question: Which category do we fall in? How should we respond to our own state of being excused by God?

Jean Valjean: The Criminal

In Victor Hugo's classic novel *Les Miserables*, the hero Jean Valjean experienced the transformation of being used. He served several years in prison for stealing bread; and upon finishing his sentence, he had no concept of what his future would yield. After staying at the bishop's home, he stole some silver and departed. The police caught him and knew the silver's origin, but the bishop did not press charges. Instead, he practiced Jesus' admonition from the Sermon on the Mount "And if someone wants to sue you and take your tunic, let him have your cloak as well" (Matt. 5:40). The bishop not only gave Jean the silverware but some candlesticks as well. Then he uttered these life-changing words, "Jean Valjean, my brother, you no longer belong to evil, but to good. It is your soul I am buying for you. I withdraw it from dark thoughts and from the spirit of perdition, and I give it to God!"[1]

Jean Valjean was at a critical point in his life in deciding how he would be used. He and the bishop both knew the devil was vying for the opportunity to use him. But God was too. And Jean had to choose whom he would serve. The bishop hoped to make the choice easier for him; and from the rest of the novel, we see that Jean Valjean did indeed make a pivotal decision at that moment. At that point he determined that he would be used as an instrument of peace, kindness and mercy.

The bishop's words to Jean Valjean were reminiscent of Paul's admonition to the Corinthians. The apostle wrote, "Do you not know that your body is a temple of the Holy Spirit, who is in you, whom you have received from God? You are not your own; you were bought at a price. Therefore honor God with your body" (1 Cor. 6:19–20). The Corinthian church was replete with sexual immorality. Paul explained to them that our bodies are vessels available for use by both God and Satan. But for Christians, the choice is clear; since our bodies no longer belong to ourselves, our bodies are vessels to be used by God. Paul confronted the Corinthians with a decision: By whom and for what would they be used?

Gomer: The Prostitute

In the Bible we have an extraordinary example of someone who is excused. The prophet Hosea was called by God to marry a prostitute named Gomer. They were married; but shortly after starting their new life together, she went back to her old ways. This marriage was a visible object lesson of a spiritual reality. It illustrated the way that God saw the people of Israel. God is eternally faithful to His people, even though they continually go after other gods. After Gomer's unfaithfulness, God said to Hosea, "Go, show your love to your wife again, though she is loved by another and is an adulteress. Love her as the Lord loves the Israelites, though they turn to other gods" (Hos. 3:1).

Not only is Gomer's unfaithfulness an example of our actions toward God, but her husband's forgiveness, longsuffering, patience and love is an example of God's actions toward us. Just as surely as Gomer was excused, so also are believers who hope in Christ excused from their sins. The Bible says, "As far as the east is from the west, so far has he removed our transgressions from us" (Ps. 103:12). With that kind of fresh start, imagine how you can be used by God!

(Exc)used, Not Excuses

I was at open house for my daughter's second grade class one time, and I perused reports on Christopher Columbus. One second grader's report began with the bold proclamation: "Christopher was a very nice man." I'm not sure how that blanket positive character reference about Christopher Columbus made it into that child's history book! I'm guessing the child did not have a great deal of information and was stretching for an extra sentence. But "nice" isn't the first thing that comes to mind when we think about the Spanish explorer, and Columbus' abuses cannot be so easily absolved by a second grader's proclamation.

When we consider that those people who have made themselves vessels for God's use are excused from their sin, we are not talking about cheap grace, God's laziness or an appeal to anyone's ignorance. Instead, we recognize that Jesus "himself bore our sins in his body on the tree [cross], so that we might die to sins and live for righteousness; by his wounds you have been healed" (1 Pet. 2:24). We make no excuses for our sin, but instead we are excused of our sin by the grace of Jesus who took our place so that we could be used by God.

To be excused of our sin, we begin with an acceptance of our wretchedness and admit that we were wrong. Admitting we are wrong goes against everything in our being, and our immature nature will put up a ridiculous fight. Once I was at dinner with a group of friends and somehow we got on the topic of temperature. Skip mentioned that the temperature in some place was fifty degrees, and immediately everyone started scoffing and ridiculing and saying it was much higher, more like eighty or ninety. Skip asserted quickly, "I meant Celsius!" The group burst into laughter, because since when would an American use Celsius? Ever since then, whenever my wife or I catch the other person saying something erroneous, the other defends, "I meant Celsius!" It's our way of laughing at our natural aversion to admitting we are wrong. The beauty of the gospel is that the admission of wrongdoing is liberating. Rather than making excuses, we can be wholly excused of our sin, simply by the grace of God.

19

(Re)used

*"I have this day lived fourscore years…God grant that I may never live
to be useless!"*

— *John Wesley*

John Wesley managed to be used by God in mighty ways.
He was the founder of the Methodist Church, a missionary to American Indians, a hymn writer, an abolitionist,
a founder of schools and orphanages, and a preacher whose
sermons are still read and studied today. He preached three
times a day, riding to each church on horseback. Clearly, he
determined that no day would be useless.

Onesimus: The Slave

One man in the Bible praised the most for his usefulness
was Onesimus. And interestingly, his name in Greek means
"useful." Paul speaks of him in the short New Testament
letter to Philemon. Onesimus was a slave (talk about being
used) who belonged to Philemon. The slave came to serve

Paul, but the letter explains that the apostle sent him back to Philemon. Paul declared in Galatians, "There is neither Jew nor Greek, slave nor free, male nor female, for you are all one in Christ Jesus" (Gal. 3:28). Paul recognized that it was not possible for a Christian to see people in unequal levels of value. The gospel makes slavery impossible, for authentic Christians will esteem others as greater than themselves, so one purpose of Paul's letter was to command Philemon to free his slave. Paul writes to the slave owner, "For this perhaps is why he was parted from you for a while, that you might have him back forever, no longer as a bondservant but more than a bondservant, as a beloved brother—especially to me, but how much more to you, both in the flesh and in the Lord. So if you consider me your partner, receive him as you would receive me" (Philem. 15–17, ESV). In other words, Paul told Philemon to receive Onesimus as a brother, rather than as a slave. Then, to make sure Philemon complied, Paul offered what can be thought of as a subtle threat: "Confident of your obedience, I write to you, knowing that you will do even more than I say" (21, ESV). Basically, Paul was saying, "I could tell you what to do. I'm your spiritual father, and you'd have to obey me. But I won't tell you what to do. Instead, I'm going to come visit you and make sure you did the right thing."

The relevance of this slave to our discussion here is his name. Of Onesimus, Paul says, "Formerly he was useless to you, but now he has become useful both to you and to me" (11). Paul recognized that we are all used by someone. As a slave, Onesimus was used by Philemon. Upon returning to Philemon, however, he could be useful to God as a free Christian.

After making a long list of the types of people who will not enter the kingdom of heaven, ranging from the sexually immoral to the greedy, Paul said, "And that is what some of you were. But you were washed, you were sanctified, you were justified in the name of the Lord Jesus Christ and by the Spirit of our God" (1 Cor. 6:11). Why Paul said, *some* of you were these things I am not sure. Perhaps he was being gracious, or perhaps he thought the list wasn't long enough to cover every human being. But the truth is that *all* of us rebel against God and are unfit for the Kingdom. Yet, like Onesimus, we have a new beginning. Like Onesimus, may it be said of each of us that though we were formerly useless, we have become useful. Though we were formerly used by the world, others and the devil, we are now vessels to be used by God.

Raskolnikov: The Murderer

In Fyodor Dostoyevsky's *Crime and Punishment*, we read of a man whose anger consumed him. In his rage he committed murder. The protagonist is Raskolnikov, an impoverished young Russian man who had to pawn his last possessions to survive. He resented the pawnbroker, an elderly woman who was not much better off than himself. His anger escalated, and over a long period of time he plotted and fantasized about murder until he finally carried out his plan. But Raskolnikov, a Christian man, knew that he had been used as an instrument of the devil to commit this crime. His conscience seared him and guilt consumed him. He eventually confided in a friend named Sonia. Her advice led to his ultimate redemption. Raskolnikov's transformational moment comes when he recognizes that he can have another chance in life. He realizes he no longer has to be used by the devil as a vessel of hate and resentment, but he can become a vessel filled with forgiveness and grace from God.

> Suddenly he remembered Sonia's words: "Go to the crossroads, bow down to the people, kiss the earth because you have sinned against it, too, and say aloud to the whole world "I am a murderer!" As he remembered, he shook all over. The blind melancholy and anxiety of the recent past, but especially of the last few hours, oppressed him to such a degree that he simply plunged into the possibility of this new, whole, and complete sensation. It came upon him suddenly like a kind of nervous fit; took fire first as a single spark in his soul, and suddenly, like flame, seized everything. Everything seemed to melt inside him, and tear flowed. He dropped to the earth where he stood . . .[1]

And Raskolnikov did exactly as Sonia prescribed. He confessed his sin, and although he was imprisoned, he went to jail with a clean conscience and without hatred or resentment. Whereas the young man was incapable of any relationships and on the verge of suicide before his confession, he found a new life in prison. Sonia moved to the same town as the prison in Siberia, and we presume that Raskolnikov was eventually released and they married.

The Bible promises that every person, no matter how sinful his or her past, can be reused in a new life with Christ. Jesus made this clear when he was at the home of Simon, and a sinful woman anointed his feet with perfume and washed them with her tears. Simon was disturbed that Jesus would associate with a woman of ill repute. He said, "If this man were a prophet, he would know who is touching him and what kind of woman she is—that she is a sinner" (Luke 7:39). But Jesus told Simon that she loved him much because she had been forgiven for much. Jesus then said to her, "Your sins are forgiven" (7:48). As surely as this woman could be reused, so can all who pour our their tears of repentance at Jesus' feet.

20

Used in Parenting

"Parenthood remains the greatest single preserve of the amateur."
—Alvin Toffler

One of the most challenging and important ways for us to be used by God is as instruments in shaping our children. Imagine how different we would approach parenting if we began each interaction with our children with the simple prayer, "God, how would you use me in the life of my child now?"

Joseph: The Hero-Dad

When I was teaching a course at Biola University, one day I came to the topic of heaven, and a student raised her hand and asked, "Will my dad get to be my dad in heaven?" That question has haunted and blessed me ever since. It blessed me because I am inspired by this man who I barely know. I am inspired by his faithfulness to his daughter and her desire to have him as a father for eternity. Her question haunted me because it set the bar frighteningly high. Would my children ask that about me? As students waited for me to answer, there must have been some who thought, *Please say no!* I don't, by the way, know the answer to that question, but I do know I aspire to be like her dad, Joseph. I hope to be worthy of my children saying the same about me.

My daughter Natasha once asked me, "Why do kids have to do what their parents say?" If I had just asked her to clean up her room, I wouldn't have found any charm in her question. But her question was sincere, so I gave it my best. I said, "God put children in families so that kids would learn what He is like. God is our Father, and we only know what that means if we have earthly fathers and mothers."

God could have designed humans another way. Many animals are born independent and don't need years of instruction. When Alaskan salmon are born they never see their mothers or fathers. They hatch from an egg and are surrounded by other hatchlings. Then they swim thousands of miles away—only to return to the very spot where they were born to spawn the next year.

God could have designed the universe in such a way that humans were born independent, but He didn't. Some people insist that speaking of God as our Father is a metaphor or an anthropomorphism (a way of explaining God in human terms). In other words, they say we are taking an image with which we are familiar to describe something unknown. We understand family structure, so we are able to apply that image as a metaphor to understand God as Father. But what if we got the metaphor backwards? What if the earthly family is God's metaphor for explaining Himself to us? That seems more likely, given that the Scriptures are a revelation from

God and not simply our best effort at describing Him. We are supposed to know what it means for God to be Father by the object lesson of our families, but perhaps the earthly family is the faulty side of the metaphor. What if God is the paradigm of a parent and He designed the earthly family as a metaphor to describe to us what He is like?

God designed us to be born as dependent children so that we would learn who He is. By seeing the mercy of our parents, we would understand his mercy. By experiencing grace from our parents, we would know His amazing grace. By receiving our parent's forgiveness, we would be assured that God is a perfect parent who also forgives us. And by living with our parents' severity and authority, we would understand what it means to submit to God "because He said so."

This understanding of parenting has a deep impact on how you will be used as a parent. Our role as parents is to represent Christ, and to reflect the image of God. This role does not induce within me pride, heavy-handedness or an authority trip. Instead, it overwhelms me with an impossible task of awesome responsibility. By my obedient actions, my children will develop an understanding of who God is. By my representation as a father, my children will know what it means for God to be their Father.

Being Used by God as a Parent

A few years ago, my son lied to me to avoid getting in trouble. Eventually he told the truth, but a struggle like that is always exhausting. It is the battle of two human wills and is evidence of a spiritual struggle as well. Shortly after the incident, I got on my bicycle and went for a ride. I spent some time in prayer, but my prayer was quite short because I was cut off by the Lord. I began, "Lord, it would have been easier if you didn't give me a child who lied. . . ." Please understand, I wasn't asking for a different kid or a different life; I was just pointing out the obvious fact that it would have been easier not to deal with lies. But in one of those few, yet strongly clear, moments when God speaks back, I heard Him distinctly say to me, "Easier for whom?"

The weight and significance of that reply has made a lasting, profound impact on *me* as a parent and also as a counselor. My plea to God implied that it would have been easier for me if my children didn't lie. But is "easiness" really relevant for my role as a parent? Isn't it more relevant to ask "Would it have been easier for my son?" If my son had been raised in another home, would his growth into a mature follower of Christ have been more likely? Perhaps God knew which home would be the easiest place for him to grow and mature, but even that is beside the point. God has a job to do. It is God's desire to raise my son into a Christlike man, and He has asked me to help Him and has put this young man on loan in my home. So the real question is, "Would it have been easier for God?" Would God's job of maturing my son have been easier if this young man were in my home or in the home of another? Since it is God's main prerogative to mature His children and since God is all-powerful and all-knowing, I trust that He made the arrangements that would suit Him best.

My role as a parent is not to raise children who make me happy. Nor is it to raise perfect children or kids who will be my lifelong friends. I realized that day on my lamenting bike ride that my role as a parent is to be used by God to carry out an important role in His task of raising His kids. So when my son lied, I was reminded of the transforming questions that are the focus of this book:

- "How will I be used as a parent?"
- "What is the purpose of this relationship?"
- "What is my role in the lives of my children?"

The Bible answers these questions for us. The Word of God explains that a parent's purpose is to be used by God to instruct his or her children.

> Hear, O Israel: The LORD our God, the LORD is one. Love the LORD your God with all your heart and with all your soul and with all your strength. These commandments that I give you today are to be upon your hearts. Impress them on your children. Talk about them when you sit at home and when you walk along the road, when you lie down and when you get up. Tie them as symbols on your hands and bind them on your foreheads. Write them on the doorframes of your houses and on your gates. (Deut. 6:4–9)

In *Shepherding a Child's Heart*, Tedd Tripp explains the connection of this passage from Deuteronomy to the task of parenting. He writes, "Whether waking, walking, talking or resting, you must be involved in helping your child to understand life, himself, and his needs from a biblical perspective."[1]

As a parent, you are God's agent in this task of providing essential training and instruction in the Lord. This does not mean you have ultimate authority; rather, you are under authority. You have a task delegated by God. You and your child are in a similar position; you both need to submit to God's authority. You have differing roles but the same master.

Tripp explains the way parents are used by God as vessels of instruction. He writes, "As a parent you have authority because God calls you to be an authority in your child's life. You have the authority to act on behalf of God. As a father or mother you do not exercise rule over your jurisdiction but over God's. You act at his command. You discharge a duty that he has given. You may not try to shape the lives of your child as pleases you, but as pleases him."[2] In other words, the role of a parent is not self-directed. Your expectations and rules are not subjective or relative. God is raising His children, perfecting and instructing them, and He has enlisted you in this task. As a parent, you are being used by God in His work of instruction.

Tripp explains how the role of a parent is delegated by God, "When you direct, correct, or discipline, you are not acting out of your own will; you are acting on behalf of God. You don't have to wonder if it is okay for you to be in charge. God has given you a duty to perform."[3]

What Parents Cannot Do

It is vital that parents be clear on their role so that they also understand what their role is not. I was slow in learning some important lessons that should have been obvious to me. For instance, I learned with my fifth child that babies prefer to be put on the changing table gently rather than plopped there. But one lesson I learned early was that I cannot control the behavior of my children.

There are some things I can do and others things that are impossible. I can tell my daughter I think she is lying. I can tell her that lying is a sin and encourage her to repent. I can tell her that she will receive a spanking or some other punishment for lying. But I cannot *make* her tell the truth.

I cannot force words to come out of her mouth; and even if I could, I would not be able to change her heart so that she had a spirit of repentance and sorrow. I suppose I could make her sit in a chair until she told the truth, but children are often able to win standoffs. My role, therefore, is not to change the behavior of my children but to speak the truth about their behavior to them. I have not been charged by God to make sure my son never lies but to instruct my son that lying is a sin and that God forgives our sins when we repent.

When I realized that I am not required to force my children to do things that are outside my control, I found peace of mind in the Serenity Prayer written by Reinhold Niebuhr: "God, grant me the serenity to accept the things I cannot change, courage to change the things I can, and wisdom to know the difference."

I cannot force my children to change, but I can instruct them. I pray for the wisdom from God to know the difference between how I can or cannot be used by Him. I know that I am not solely responsible for their actions, but I am responsible for speaking the truth to them about their actions. As a parent, you are used by God as a vessel of truth to your children.

21

Used in Marriage

"Marriage is our last, best chance to grow up."
—Joseph Barth

The dedication at the beginning of this book reads, "For my wife Kristina, whom God has used as His primary instrument in shaping me." Marriage is God's most efficient tool of shaping us into His image. Imagine if we approached every difficult marital interaction with this simple prayer, "God, how would you use me in the life of my spouse?"

Jen: Always Late

Keith's wife is often late, and this gets on his nerves. He says he does not want or expect to change his wife, Jen. He's often heard the advice that you don't go into marriage trying to change someone. But because he makes comments from time to time about her being late, she can tell that he really does see her tardiness as a character flaw.

He has employed various strategies to communicate his irritation with her being late. He tried to set her clock fast, he set the alarm on her cell phone, he wrote reminders, etc. He would make comments like, "I'm going to be on time, how about you?" And he would drive separate cars to the same destination, just to make sure that he wouldn't be late.

The persistent tardiness after twenty years of marriage dumbfounds him in light of how often he has communicated irritation and despite all his creative attempts. He has addressed Jen's late arrivals subtly, directly, sarcastically—yet still there has been no change. Clearly, Jen's tardiness will not be solved by better education or communication. What Keith doesn't realize is that Jen has subconsciously figured out that Keith is not only irritated with her being late but that he has some contempt for her. She didn't ask him to set the alarm, speed up the watch or write the notes. She has never, in fact, asked for his help in getting her somewhere on time. She does not value prompt arrivals. She is actually quite comfortable with her lifestyle, and she usually arrives at places the time that she had hoped to; but to tell this to Keith would exacerbate the contempt that she already knows he has. She lets him believe that she is trying harder so she doesn't have to deal with the contempt.

At the core of Keith and Jen's issue is confusion over their purpose in marriage. Their marriage is on the verge of a life-changing transformation if they can answer these questions:

- "How will I be used in the life of my spouse?"
- "What is the purpose of this relationship?"
- "Why does God have me in this marriage?"

Keith and Jen were unclear about their role in each other's lives, so they let certain assumptions about that purpose develop implicitly over time. To some extent, Keith came to see his role as parental. In other words, he implicitly believed that his role was to help Jen make better decisions and to develop mature character traits.

People will supply various answers, even somewhat biblical answers, to the question, "What is the purpose of marriage?" Glancing at the account of Adam and Eve, some might assume that the husband's role is to provide financially since God told Adam that he would work the ground, and by his sweat, it would produce. Likewise some might assume that Eve's role is to bear children since God told Eve that she would have pain in childbirth. This answer might seem satisfactory since it appears so early in the history of humankind and in the Bible (see Gen. 3:16–19). But this early passage of Scripture does not tell us what the husband's and wife's role is in each other's lives.

That answer is found even earlier, in Genesis 1:27: "So God created man in his own image, in the image of God he created him; male and female he created them." The role of the husband is to be the image of God to his wife. The role of the wife is to be the image of God to her husband. Together, the two are the image of God. It is not Keith's role to parent his wife, but instead to be the image of God and to be one with his wife. To answer the questions above then, we might say:

- The purpose of marriage is to be the image of God to/with another person and to become "one."
- God has me in this marriage to show my spouse what God is like.

- I will be used by God to speak the truth about who God is and what God desires.

The Purpose of Marriage

Because marriage can be difficult, people tend to set the bar low for their goals. I asked one man what his goal for his marriage was and he said, "Not to have any bickering this week." Ironically, by setting the bar low, we will never achieve it. That's because our low goals are essentially self-serving, but marriage is designed to be an other-serving arrangement. So as long as our goals are wrong, no matter how low they may be, we will never achieve them because marriage is designed for another purpose.

In his book *The Marriage Builder*, Larry Crabb addresses the purpose of marriage. Crabb writes that the goal of marriage is to develop "a deep experience of personal intimacy through relationship with a person of the opposite sex."[1] This goal is relentlessly other-centered, but it is not self-deprecating. In other words, both partners have much to gain by self-sacrifice. Crabb encourages, "Commit yourself to ministering to your spouse's needs, knowing that however he may respond can never rob you of your worth as a person."[2]

The purpose of marriage, in other words, is to be used by God as an instrument of discipleship for your spouse. Crabb writes about his relationship with his wife, "I regard it as part of my role as spiritual leader to help her do the best job she can as wife and mother."[3] The purpose of marriage is not primarily for our own happiness or satisfaction. Neither is it primarily for the happiness or satisfaction of our spouse. Marriage fits a purpose within God's plan. The purpose of marriage is that the two partners will be vessels for use by God in His task of perfecting His children (you and your spouse).

Marriage, in this sense, is a ministry. It is ministry through intimacy, which Crabb calls "Soul Oneness." He explains, "The key to achieving Soul Oneness is to maintain the fundamental goal of ministry to our partner's deepest needs and to keep that goal inviolate."[4] For a successful marriage, each day we must remind ourselves that we can be used by God in the life of our partner. Crabb summarizes this role, "Husbands and wives are to regard marriage as an opportunity to minister in a unique and special way to another human being, to be used of God to bring their spouses into a more satisfying appreciation of their worth as persons who are secure and significant in Jesus Christ."[5]

I mentioned earlier that Keith was confused about his role in his wife's life. If he is clear that his role is to reflect the image of God, how would he address his wife's tardiness? Let me offer a suggestion of what he could say: "Jen, I believe that other people are honored when we arrive on time. Showing up on time is something I value, and I think we should get better at it. I imagine that you are less pressured to be on time because you value something else, and I would like to understand it. How do you feel about being late? Is there something else that is more important for you?"

If Keith says something like this to his wife, he has accomplished two things. First, he has reflected the image of God. He has graciously and lovingly spoken the truth about the situation. Second, he has expressed to his wife how much he values intimacy (knowing her) even more than being on time. He has begun a conversation that will help him know his wife better, which is the purpose of marriage (oneness).

In marriage we can be used by God to reflect His image. We do this by speaking and acting the way that God does. God does not force us to act differently, and we are not able to force our spouse to act differently either. But God does speak the truth about our behavior. And we can speak the truth to our spouse about how we feel or what we believe. When we do that, we leave the results in God's hands, content that we have been used by Him.

22

Used for Intimacy

"Society, dead or alive, can have no charm without intimacy, and no intimacy without an interest in trifles."

—*Arthur James Balfour*

Intimacy is a much broader concept than sexual activity. Intimacy is "knowing." God put within us a deep desire to know and to be known. We derive our satisfaction from relationships by building this kind of intimacy. Since sexual activity involves a vulnerable and private part of our lives, it is a concrete example of knowing, or intimacy, but it is only one example among many relational facets of intimacy. God uses us in the lives of others to build intimacy.

Jerry: The Sarcastic Husband

Jerry and his wife, Melissa, were discussing with me a recent disagreement. They live near Disneyland, where many people have annual passes and special discounts for being local residents. Melissa said that because of financial problems, she was thinking of getting the lowest level of passes, which would restrict them from going to the park on weekends. Jerry shook his head and said, "That's the first I ever heard of that." It was obvious that he was against the idea. I could see that I was about to get my own free ticket to an attraction—a fight—but it wouldn't be amusing. I said to Jerry, "Your goal is not to get the better passes to Disneyland." Jerry was confused; "It's not?" I could tell he was pretty sure I was wrong. I said, "Your goal is intimacy with your wife. If you try to prove your case, both of you will dig in your heels and become defensive. Use this opportunity to know your wife. See it the way she sees it. Ask her why she wants these passes, what it would mean for her if you didn't get them, and what she is afraid will happen. Get into her world and know her."

Jerry and Melissa need to ask a basic question, which is, "What is the purpose of this relationship?" Is the purpose to save money, enjoy entertainment, overcome loneliness? When we are clear about the purpose of the relationship, many of the other issues become clear as well. When we affirm that the purpose of marriage is to build intimacy, then we are mindful that disagreements are opportunities to know the other person better. When Jerry and Melissa asked God what the purpose of their relationship was, they learned that they could be used by God as vessels of intimacy for one another.

The idea that the primary purpose of marriage is intimacy is made clear in the beginning of the Bible. We read in Genesis 4:1, "Adam lay with his wife Eve, and she conceived." It's no surprise that Adam lay with his wife or that sexual union has been central to marriage since the beginning. But interestingly, the word translated "lay with" is the Hebrew word *Yada*. Literally, *Yada* means "to know." If you read Genesis 4:1 in the King James Version, it says, "And Adam knew Eve his wife; and she conceived." Both translations of *Yada* are accurate. The general word "to know" is often the one supplied for sex. This is not merely a euphemism; there's plenty of explicit material in the Bible to show the biblical authors didn't have qualms about the precise words for sex. When sex is equated with "to know," it is because the concepts are similar in the mind of the author. Sex is a way to know someone, to create intimacy.

Jan: The Frustrated Daughter

Intimacy is not only for marriage. It is a worthy goal in every relationship. Jan is an adult woman living with her mother. Her mother struggles with OCD (obsessive-compulsive disorder). Because of her condition, their relationship can be quite strained and is far from ideal or even typical. Jan told me that her mother often takes the things that she buys for herself like food, toiletries, etc., and doesn't replace them. Jan felt violated and hopeless that anything would change, even with confrontation. Generous people tolerate a certain degree of this behavior; but it can be frustrating when there is no reciprocation, acknowledgement of the problem, gratitude or warning.

I encouraged Jan that she may have misjudged the purpose of her relationship at this point with her mother. When she was a child, the purpose of the relationship was for her mother to care for and raise her. Now that she is an adult, Jan said she thought her current purpose was to be a good daughter. I suggested that throughout the stages of life, there are changes in the purpose of a mother/daughter relationship.

Perhaps her current purpose is to serve her mother. Maybe it is to care for her as she struggles with her disorder. Or maybe God's purpose is for her to know herself better. The ideal purpose for the relationship is for Jan and her mother to gain intimacy as friends.

Jan is going to be perpetually frustrated if she does not know why God is using her in that relationship. Once she gains clarity on that question, she will have a way to deal with what is happening when she is violated in some way by her mother. In those situations, she can ask, "How does God want to use me in this relationship?" Then, rather than react as a victim, she can act intentionally as a vessel of God.

23

Used for Racial Reconciliation

*"And he made from one man every nation of mankind
to live on all the face of the earth."*

Acts 17:26, ESV

Many of our most prominent heroes are those who have been instrumental in building racial reconciliation: Martin Luther King, Gandhi, Nelson Mandela, etc. But problems with racial division are as old as history. God used people throughout the Bible to promote racial reconciliation—most notably the apostle Paul who showed that the gospel of salvation was for people of all ethnic groups. There is no reason to leave this work to heroes who will be remembered throughout history; God can use you too as an instrument of racial reconciliation.

Elton: The Reconciler

Elton is an elderly friend of mine who lives off the land. He goes to the grocery store just a few times a year, instead feeding himself and his wife with hunted game, homegrown produce, trapped animals and roadkill. I know this because I provided one of the animals from roadkill for him. In contrast to Elton, I grew up in the suburbs. One of the differences between our upbringings was attitudes toward race. In my suburban environment, if people were racist, they kept their thoughts to themselves. Even bigoted people knew that it was inappropriate to openly voice prejudiced remarks. But Elton lives in a part of the country where racist comments were sometimes publicly tolerated. He is not only old enough to remember the civil rights movement; he lives in a community where the struggle continues.

For the most part, Elton and his wife keep to themselves, but they often invite us to have lunch at their home after church. I was surprised when they invited two young black men from Kenya—who were hoping to qualify as runners in the Olympics through a program at a local university— to lunch with us one week. I've never known Elton to be so hospitable—to someone like me, yes, but never to these two young men. I thought, *Maybe Elton has changed.* I drove these young men and Elton in my Jeep with the top off on a beautiful spring afternoon. Elton sat in the front, and the two visitors were in the back. As the four of us were cruising down the country roads, Elton said to me, "Pull over. I can't be seen with these black men in the back." I was pretty shocked. Why would he have gotten in the car in the first place if this was such a problem? He must have seen the bewilderment on my face, and he explained, "One of them must move up front. We can't have the black men sitting in the back." I have never forgotten Elton's surprisingly new passion for racial sensitivity—nor how he struggled to get

152

into the back of my Jeep. Elton had changed. He saw these men as men, and it was important to him that they were publically respected. Despite living in a community where subtle and not-so-subtle racism was the norm, Elton allowed God to change his heart. Even as an older man, his attitude toward race changed. At some point in his life, Elton must have said to himself, "I will be used as a vehicle for racial reconciliation."

The Early Christians and Racial Reconciliation

The apostle Paul also had a moment where his identity was transformed and he made an explicit decision to be used for racial reconciliation. Before Paul's conversion, almost no one had become a Christian without either being Jewish or becoming Jewish in the process. So the early church was confused about what to do with new Christians who were not Jewish— those called Gentiles. They wondered if the Gentiles should convert to Judaism as part of their conversion, as many had not yet envisioned that Christianity was a different religion than Judaism. But Paul quickly became convinced that Gentiles could and would be saved without becoming Jewish or adopting the Jewish customs and laws. The transformational moment came when Paul began preaching to the Gentiles and left the other apostles to preach to the Jews. Paul said, "And for this purpose I was appointed a herald and an apostle—I am telling the truth, I am not lying—and a teacher of the true faith to the Gentiles" (1 Tim. 2:7). In the letters to the Galatians and the Romans, Paul called himself "an apostle to the Gentiles." It was Paul who declared, "There is neither Jew nor Greek, slave nor free, male nor female, for you are all one in Christ Jesus" (Gal. 3:28). Paul made a clear commitment to being used as a bridge between two opposing ethnic groups (Jews and Gentiles) as well as to eliminating all other causes of division such as class (slave or free) and gender.

With this precedent, Christians are clearly called to be used by God as tools for reconciliation of all kinds. But this reconciliation is not a simple naïve wish, nor is it rooted in a vain hope in humanity. Instead, the rationale for reconciliation is the humble admission that we are all in the same fallen condition and are all in need of the same Savior. As we point people to Him, we are used by God as tools of peace.

24

Used to Confront

"Faithful are the wounds of a friend."
Proverbs 27:6

We often create artificial harmony in public and then air our grievances privately when the person offending us is not around. But Jesus counseled us to take our grievances directly to the person who sinned against us (see Matt. 18). Sometimes we take this responsibility with pride and excess, forgetting our dependence on the Holy Spirit and our own fallen state (see chapter 11). But occasionally we feel particularly equipped and called by the Holy Spirit to be used by God as a tool of confrontation.

Kristina: The Prophet

My wife and I were moving across the country with everything we had in a U-Haul, and we stopped for dinner at a fast-food restaurant. Seated in the booth next to us were three people whose conversation we could not help but overhear.

There were two men and a woman, all who seemed to be in their sixties. It was clear from their conversation that they had just come from a Sunday night church gathering where a missionary had spoken. Their conversation went something like this:

> "Why did Pastor have to use that overhead projector? Doesn't he know we can't see that thing?"

> "Why did they play that loud music? It's unbearable!"

> "Why did that missionary speak in another language? Can't he tell we all speak English. He went on speaking gibberish, and I couldn't tell a word of it."

> "That service was way too long. We should have been out of there an hour before that was done. Were all those pictures really necessary?"

Because my wife is strongly introverted, you can imagine my shock when she got up and went over to their table. She politely said in an unassuming voice, "I could not help but hear your conversation, and it seems to me that you are more concerned about what you want than about what God wants." One of the men sitting at the table was cut to the heart and he said humbly, "You're probably right." The woman next to him defiantly said, "Well, to each his own."

As we listened to this conversation, my wife was confronted with a decision: How would she be used by God? She could have listened silently and harbored judgment or let anger well up, as this experience reminded her of past incidents where she or I were the object of gossip. She could have ignored the whole thing and blew the neighbors off, either because it was not a big deal or because the gossipers were a lost cause. But instead, she decided to be used by God as an instrument of correction.

The Bible exhorts us to be such an instrument in the lives of others. We read, "And let us consider how we may spur one another on toward love and good deeds. Let us not give up meeting together, as some are in the habit of doing, but let us encourage one another—and all the more as you see the Day approaching"(Heb. 10:24–25).

Calculating Confrontation

The Bible doesn't state that we have the luxury of calculating whether our rebuke, admonition or correction is going to be well-received or successful. Though the outcome will vary, there is a constant place for God's people to be used as instruments of encouragement and correction.

Peter, a husband and father of three sons in our church struggled daily with a drinking problem. His close friends spoke to him privately, and then they asked the elders of the church to meet with him to express our concern for him and his family. Peter admitted his struggle, wept, asked for help and repented. We set up a schedule for men in the church to call him every morning to encourage him and ask how the previous day went. Though Peter originally was overcome with tears, admission and sorrow, his behavior never changed. Eventually his wife filed for divorce, he lost custody of his children, and he lost his job and home. The rebuke was initially well-received, but ultimately there was not a successful outcome. Neither of these two points is relevant, however, to whether the elders of the church did the right thing. We can't concern ourselves with the chances of success or the likely reaction of the other person. We concern ourselves with our role as vessels of use by God.

On a similar occasion, a group of women from our church met with an elderly, single woman named Gail who was also struggling with alcoholism. Many were doubtful that Gail had any chance of kicking the habit she had practiced for several decades, and some assumed that she would be bitter about the subject. Yet Gail also responded with contrition; and with God's help, she maintained a sober life after that event.

Neither the chance of success nor the person's likely response should deter us from exhortation when it is needed. The Bible says, "If you see the donkey of someone who hates you fallen down under its load, do not leave it there; be sure you help him with it" (Exod. 23:5). If we are expected to help an enemy in need, how much more a friend! Your friends are not in need of a rebuke every time you disagree with them, but there may be a few occasions in your life when you realize that you can be used by God to correct and hopefully rescue a friend from sin.

Taking Correction Too Far

Some people think that correction or rebuke is always judgmental and is, therefore, not Christian behavior. They appeal to the Sermon on the Mount where Jesus said, "How can you say to your brother, 'Let me take the speck out of your eye,' when all the time there is a plank in your own eye?" (Matt. 7:4). It is wise to take from this passage a charge to be humble and consider your own faults. But notice that Jesus didn't say, "Never take out a neighbor's speck." To ignore the speck would be unloving. The call is not to silence, but to humble, careful, loving correction.

Of course, not everyone has mastered the perfect, gracious rebuke. Our youth were at a summer camp for a week in the mountains. Jake, a recent high school graduate, joined us as a counselor. He was raised in a tidy home and always practiced excellent hygiene. He must have been the only tidy one in the group, however, because he became incensed at the mess in the bathroom and especially the ever-present urine on the toilet seat. Finally he picked out who he thought was the primary culprit. He bought some Depends from the pharmacy and wrote "Do not pee on the seat" on a pair. Then he put the garment on the young man while he was sleeping. I hope we can agree that this was not what Paul meant by "speaking the truth in love" (Eph. 4:15).

Because examples of haughty or harsh rebuke abound, some doubt whether a loving admonition is possible. I can assure you from experience that some have mastered the perfect rebuke—for I have given them the opportunity to practice. One Sunday morning I showed a brief YouTube clip from *Monty Python and the Holy Grail* (the black knight scene). I previewed it several times, but the quality was poor enough that I didn't notice a curse at the end of the scene. After this event, Chuck, a respected teacher in our church, spoke with me. He said, "I believe that you were well-intentioned and that you don't want any profanity in church. I was offended, and I think we should avoid things like this in the future." Through that rebuke, Chuck was supportive and he believed the best. He represented himself and not the feelings of others. He came to me rather than gossiping with someone else. He expressed the way he felt and what he wanted done in the future rather than dwelling on the past. Paul wrote, "Let the word of Christ dwell in you richly as you teach and admonish one another with all wisdom, and as you sing psalms, hymns and spiritual songs with gratitude in your hearts to God" (Col. 3:16). With that rebuke, Chuck admonished me with wisdom.

When my twin brother and I were teenagers, we both watched a violent R-rated movie. I can't remember the title, but I remember our conversation afterward. He said, "Dan, we are on a quest for holiness." At that moment I made a decision that I would more carefully guard my movie intake and, except in rare, justified occasions, not watch any R-rated movies. What makes the event most memorable is the grace with which my brother rebuked me. He used words like "us," rather than accusing just me; and he spoke of the direction we were going, rather than just looking at the past. He spoke with hope and love. This is what David Augsburger calls "care-fronting."

> Care-fronting is offering genuine caring that bids another to grow. Care-fronting is offering real confrontation that calls out new insight and understanding. Care-fronting unites love and power. So one can have something to stand for (goals) as well as someone to stand with (relationship) without sacrificing one for the other.[1]

Jesus told us that we can be used by God to give a loving rebuke. He said, "If your brother sins against you, go and show him his fault, just between the two of you. If he listens to you, you have won your brother over" (Matt. 18:15). The purpose of this rebuke is not to prove yourself better than other people, destroy other people or end your relationship with other people. The purpose of the rebuke, as Jesus said above, is to "win your brother over." You can be used by God to win a brother back to fellowship with God.

25

Used to Give

"It is better to suffer wrong than to do it, and happier to be sometimes cheated than not to trust."

—Samuel Johnson

It's often said that we are born into this world clenching our fists and we leave this world with our hands wide open. In other words, we spend most of our lives trying to grab hold of more stuff, only to leave it all behind when we die. It's not just "stuff" we are grabbing more of—we want more power, more prestige, more honor, more pleasure, more time, more whatever. When my nephew was three years old, he understood this well. He had apparently been asking for M&M's at various times, to which his parents responded, "You'll choke." Eventually, he shortcut the whole interchange by simply exclaiming, "I want to choke! I want to choke!" And who doesn't? We want stuff—no matter what it is or what the effects are. We want so much of it that we want to be choked by it. But God knows that the opposite is better for us. He wants to use us as instruments of giving.

Cheryl: The Giver

My friend Cheryl has a trademark expression: "It's only money." She has always been clear that money is a tool to be used by God. She refuses to allow herself to be a slave to money. The majority of us, however, have what must seem to God like an insane preoccupation with money. If we see money as a tool, rather than an end in itself, the idea that "it's only money" is a helpful reminder. It puts the purpose of money in proper perspective and makes giving it away easier.

Cheryl's brother Victor disappeared and became estranged from her family when he was in his twenties. Since they didn't hear from him for decades, they weren't sure what happened and had given up hope of hearing from him again. He reappeared in their lives when he was in his sixties, with no particular explanation of where he had been or what had happened. When Cheryl reconnected with Victor, it was apparent he had a high level of paranoia about the government. Somehow he now owns a home in the desert, but he tries to stay "off the grid" as much as possible. A neighbor lets him put a garden hose through the window so he doesn't have to get a water bill. He won't pay his property taxes, but Uncle Sam won't let Victor get away with that. So when Cheryl heard that this situation would likely result in a recurrence of Victor's homelessness, she acted with radical generosity. She bought his house and became responsible for the property taxes. She said, "It's only money." She understood that as a vessel designed for God's use, her money also serves the same purpose.

We don't always see money in this way. As a teenager, I often went off-roading in my Jeep with friends. My friend Brian was driving ahead of me on an American Indian reservation, and I gave him some room because he was kicking up a lot of dust and I knew he was driving too fast. He rounded a corner where I lost sight of him, but I saw a large cloud of dust emerge in the air. When I caught up, I saw that he had rolled his truck but, thankfully, was fine. He crawled out of the passenger window; and when he was upright, he said, "My life is over," because his truck was ruined. In retrospect that was clearly an overstatement, but it is a worldview that we often have toward our possessions. Loosening our grip on money feels like losing our life. For some this becomes a consistent attitude toward money. Rather than using money, money uses them. Such people have decided that they will use money to give them pleasure and security; but by using money in this way, they are being used by money. Money has become their master.

This is not the only option. Jesus said, "No servant can serve two masters. Either he will hate the one and love the other, or he will be devoted to the one and despise the other. You cannot serve both God and Money" (Luke 16:13). Some people have determined that they will not be used by money; instead, they and their money will be used by God.

My wife works with a teacher who struggled with infertility. This teacher and her husband wanted a child, and indicated that they wanted to try in vitro fertilization (IVF) but knew the cost was prohibitive. Incredibly, another teacher was sympathetic to their grief and offered to pay the $15,000 to make IVF possible. We live among such people who are able to view their money and themselves as vehicles of blessing. Their money has a purpose, as do they—to be used by God.

When we grasp that the purpose of money is to be used by God, we are able to make decisions with extreme abandon. The apostle Paul wrote, "The very fact that you have lawsuits among you means you have been completely defeated already. Why not rather be wronged? Why not rather be cheated?" (1 Cor. 6:7). This question has an obvious answer. Why not rather be wronged or cheated? Because it hurts! Because it makes me mad! Because it's wrong! These are all true responses.

In order to be used by God, we must loosen the grasp that money has on us. Believe it or not, some people have done this with extraordinary success. In fact, some people would even find our love of money bizarre. My twin brother, Ken, lived in a primitive island village with his wife and four kids for ten years completing a translation of the New Testament. They lived about as primitive as you can get—no running water, no power, no stores for supplies. After two years, my wife and I planned a visit, so my brother told the village we were coming. A man in the village warned Ken, "Your brother will cry when he sees how you live." Now you and I are thinking, *How sad! They are so destitute that they assume we would cry to see how they live.* But in reality, the villager meant, *When your brother sees how easy life is here—how you don't work the soil, how you pull food off the trees, how you enjoy the days under the sun—he will cry out of jealousy.*

It is possible for us to be used by God, but we cannot be used by money at the same time. Jesus said, "You cannot serve both God and Money" (Matt. 6:24). There are good reasons to prevent someone from wronging or cheating you. There are good reasons to seek compensation and justice. But there are also opportunities for us to be used by God as vessels of grace. We can make the conscious decision to allow ourselves to be wronged, and to sacrifice for another. When we make this decision, we experience the joy of being used by God to give.

26

Used to Bear Burdens

"We are all here on earth to help others; what on earth the others are here for I don't know."

—W.H. Auden

The apostle Paul wrote, "Carry each other's burdens, and in this way you will fulfill the law of Christ" (Gal. 6:2). Sometimes the burdens that people carry are emotional, and we can be used by God to share that burden. Sometimes the burden is financial, and our gifts can be used by God to alleviate the difficulty. Sometimes the burden is physical, and we can be used by God to lend a hand.

Emotional Burdens

A few years ago my family was driving in our old RV through Durango, Colorado. On that particular trip we tried to keep costs down by staying in the driveways of people we knew or on undeveloped government land, called BLM land (Bureau of Land Management). In Durango we saw a BLM

167

office on the highway, so I decided to pop inside and ask the agent if there was some place we could stay the night for free. The agent got the question right but apparently got the wrong idea, because he said, "Yeah, my heart really goes out to guys like you. I was living on the streets for ten years. And you just want to find an overpass to sleep under or some place to stay for the night that the police won't hassle you." It wasn't particularly important for me to correct the guy's impression, and he gave me the information I needed. I was deeply moved by his immediate empathy for another person. My problem became his problem. Some people are like that. They have made a decision that when they sense someone else in need, they will try to see themselves as part of the solution.

This can be overdone and, in fact, lead to an unhealthy sense of self-importance, as well as to the condition of co-dependence. My wife and I have adopted two children; but when we see images of international poverty, we both have a sense that we should do more to help. There can actually be a form of idolatry in this. If in every situation I believe that I am needed, I become God. And if in every situation my money is needed, then my money becomes God. The goal is not to *do* something every time I see a need, but instead to be *available* for God to use me every time He opens my eyes to a need. Moses only saw one burning bush in his life. He did not try to set the Israelites free from Pharaoh before that point. But when the invitation from God came, he was ready and available to respond. I don't want to act presumptuously as if I am God's solution to every problem, but I do want to be used by God when He invites me to do so.

Physical Burdens

A few years ago, I planned a backpacking trip for the young adults of our church to the highest mountain in the country, Mount Whitney. We intended to hike twenty-four miles over five days; so I promised that the trip would not be extremely strenuous, even though the altitude would be high. We had about fifteen youth or college students in the group, and most were inexperienced. Unfortunately, I was not able to obtain the permit to enter the trailhead at the shortest route, so we had to turn the trip into a fifty-five mile hike or abandon the hope of reaching the summit. The group decided to make the trek; but by the time we were nearing the summit on the fourth day, most were struggling. We were, however, at the point of no return as the shortest way home had become over the trail crest near the summit. Nearly every hiker was sick and exhausted, but we had to move higher. Sean, a new Christian, realized the severity of the situation; so he hiked fast to the top, dropped his pack and ran back to us. Then he grabbed the pack of the next person he saw, carried it to the top and ran back again. That day he carried five people's packs to the highest point of the trail and hiked several miles further than anyone else. His enthusiasm and determination were contagious, and the remaining healthy people came back for other packs when they reached the top. Sean put into practice Paul's charge to, "Carry each other's burdens." He realized that he could be used by God literally to carry other people's loads.

In the Boy Scouts there is an auxiliary organization for older boys called the "Order of the Arrow." As young men are initiated into this group, they enact a ceremony that puts into practice the concept of bearing other people's burdens.

The guys form two lines facing each other, and the first person on one side lifts a very heavy brick to his shoulder. Then the leader says, "Let no one pass the burden to his brother, yet bear it until it is lifted from his shoulder." In this ceremony the youth enact a biblical principle. Rather than pass their burdens or bear them alone, brothers come to their aid and lift the burdens from their shoulders.

As Christians, we often wait until someone asks us to carry the burden or until the burden, falls or gets passed to us. But if we identify ourselves as God's vessels, available for use, we will see the burdens and will not wait for them to be passed.

27

Used to Comfort

"Ill news hath wings, and with the wind doth go,
Comfort's a cripple and comes ever slow."

—*Michael Drayton in* The Barons' Wars

We read in Paul's letter to the Corinthians, "[God] comforts us in all our affliction, so that we may be able to comfort those who are in any affliction, with the comfort with which we ourselves are comforted" (2 Cor. 1:4, ESV). God enables us to be used as a vessel of comfort. Comfort can mean a variety of things: a warm meal, a night's rest, an encouraging word, a shoulder to cry on or a promise of assistance. Consider how you can be used by God to comfort others.

Douglas: The Transformed Workaholic

When I was the pastor of a church in rural Indiana, there were many lifelong members in the church. Much of the church was comprised of several generations belonging to a few families. One pillar of the church, Douglas, was the president of a large company. He was, by every definition, a workaholic. There were nights he stayed at the office, and some Sunday mornings I noticed him dozing during my sermon—which could *only* be explained by not having enough sleep the night before. Clearly, his work was a high priority for him. But years later I found out just how high a priority his family was to him.

After finishing seminary, my wife and I moved back to California, but we returned to this midwestern church ten years later. When I saw Douglas again, I was eager to find out what he had been up to, and I assumed he was working harder than ever. I asked, "What have you been doing for the last year?" His answer struck me with awe. He said, "I have been lying on the floor next to my father's bed. His health has been failing, so I have been caring for him at night." At some point in Douglas' life, he made a decision about how he would be used. He would not be used by a company. He would not be used by money. And once retired, his time would not be used simply for his own pleasure. Instead, he said to God, "I will be used as an instrument of care."

Charity: The Sister

In Herman Melville's classic, *Moby Dick*, the praises are sung of a woman named Charity who was passionate about meeting the needs of others.

> Chief among those who did this fetching and carrying was Captain Bildad's sister, a lean old lady of a most determined and indefatigable spirit, but withal very kindhearted, who seemed resolved that, if she could help it, nothing should be found wanting in the Pequod, after once fairly getting to sea. At one time she would come

on board with a jar of pickles for the steward's pantry; another time with a bunch of quills for the chief mate's desk, where he kept his log; a third time with a roll of flannel for the small of some one's rheumatic back. Never did any woman better deserve her name, which was Charity—Aunt Charity, as everybody called her. And like a sister of charity did this charitable Aunt Charity bustle about hither and thither, ready to turn her hand and heart to anything that promised to yield safety, comfort, and consolation to all on board a ship in which her beloved brother Bildad was concerned.[1]

Charity made a decision that she would only be used as a vessel of comfort and for meeting the needs of others. The Bible tells us that God is also involved in the ministry of comfort. Paul writes, "Praise be to the God and Father of our Lord Jesus Christ, the Father of compassion and the God of all comfort, who comforts us in all our troubles, so that we can comfort those in any trouble with the comfort we ourselves have received from God" (2 Cor. 1:3–4). As vessels for God's use, we can employ the same ministry of comfort for others.

28

Used to Encourage

"But encourage one another daily, as long as it is called 'Today,' so that none of you may be hardened by sin's deceitfulness."

Hebrews 3:13

I love Hebrews 3:13 because as far as I know, every day is called "today," so we will be encouraging one another for a long time! One simple way you can be used by God, that costs you little time and effort, is as a tool of encouragement.

Sarah: The Encourager

A girl named Sarah was paid the greatest compliment by her grandfather that I imagine anyone could receive. He said, "I feel like a better person when I am around her." I hope you are fortunate to know someone like that. There is a certain breed of people, extraordinary people, from whose lips encouragement ceaselessly falls. Sarah is like that. She tells the people around her that they're wonderful, loved and valuable. It seems as if each morning she makes a decision to let her tongue be used to build rather than destroy.

We live a quarter mile away from our kids' school. Nevertheless, that short amount of time is enough for an incredible amount of verbal poison. One day, after only being awake for a few minutes and after hearing my kids tear each other down, I demanded that they only say encouraging things to one other. Result: they were silent. I was terrified, however, at the thought that this may have been asking the impossible. They were so out of exercise in the gift of encouragement that there was no well from which to draw any fresh affirmation. Had someone just made a goal in soccer, they could have said, "Good job." But since they had only been awake for a few minutes, they had not been witness to any goals and therefore had no reservoir of ideas. We actually had to take some time to write a list of things one could say to encourage the other, even if you just awakened and had not witnessed any accomplishments. (Just in case you're drawing a blank, the list included things like "Have a good day," "I hope you do well in school" and "Would you like me to carry your backpack?")

I attended a recognition ceremony for an adult who volunteered with youth. Those recognizing him made a carefully prepared speech after consulting with numerous friends and colleagues about his character. From the praise of several friends emerged a common theme. Those honoring him said, "His most common words are please and thank you." This particular organization has a strong American Indian heritage, so when they offered his award, they chose a new Indian name for him—one that meant "encourager."

There is a big difference between the words "admire" and "aspire." When we admire someone, we like what she is doing, but we have no intent of doing the same. For example, everyone admired Mother Teresa, but few wanted to work with the dying like she did. But when we aspire, we like what someone is doing enough that we want to be like him. When I heard the praise given to Mr. Encourager, I aspired to be like him. "May the words of my mouth and the meditation of my heart be pleasing in your sight, O Lord" (Ps. 19:14). I want to be used by God as a voice of encouragement.

In the Bible we learn of a man named Barnabas who determined to be used by God as an encourager. His birth name was Joseph; but the apostles renamed him Barnabas, which means "Son of Encouragement" (Acts 4:36). The renaming of this man is inspiring to me, because it makes me wonder what character trait I have expressed overtly enough to justify a name change.

Many of us have coworkers or friends who often complain about their spouse or their boss. These complainers seem to have support because few people confront them; but silently, the people around them are exhausted, and the complaints backfire without the complainers knowing it. Their friends inwardly think less of them. On the other hand, I know a woman who has earned the reputation of always saying encouraging things to her coworkers about her husband whom they have never met. Interestingly, not only do her coworkers have a heroic view of her husband, they have an even higher regard for her. Everyone wants to be around an encourager.

The Bible encourages us to be such people. The apostle Paul wrote, "Therefore encourage one another and build each other up, just as in fact you are doing" (1 Thess. 5:11).

You can be used by God as a vessel of encouragement. When you are, you will be meeting a God-given need within the lives of the people around you. Authors John Trent and Gary Smalley contend that there is a "universal quest for a blessing." Everyone has a profound need to be affirmed, encouraged and blessed by the words of another. Trent and Smalley write, "For almost all children who miss out on their parents' blessing, at some level this lack of acceptance sets off a lifelong search."[1] You can be used by God to help people find what they are looking for, whether you provide the verbal blessing for a spouse, child, friend, coworker, neighbor or stranger. Trent and Smalley contend that the need for encouragement goes largely unmet. They write, "The same painful cry and unfulfilled longing is being echoed today by many people who are searching for their family's blessing, men and women whose parents, for whatever reason, have failed to bless them with words of love and acceptance."[2]

As a vessel of God, you can meet this need. Speaking particularly to parents, Smalley and Trent say, "If you are a parent, learning about the family blessing can help you provide your child(ren) with a protective tool."[3] But the verbal blessing is not limited to families. Regardless of who you are used by God to encourage, Trent and Smalley offer five ways to bless others. First, they suggest that meaningful touch is a way to pass on a blessing. Throughout Scripture we see the laying on of hands as a form of bestowing a blessing. Second, they recommend a spoken message where you affirm the other person. Third, they remind you to attach high value to the person you are blessing and to speak of their worth—not what they have done, but who they are. Fourth, they say that a blessing invokes the picture of a special future. Affirm out loud specifically what you wish to see happen to the person you are encouraging. Last, Trent and Smalley say that a blessing involves an active commitment to the other person.

Consider how you will be used by God to encourage. God will give you opportunities today where you see a person in need of a blessing.

29

Used to Take Risks

"We are constantly at risk from the people we love most. They are, after all, the only people who can do us serious damage."

—Jennifer Johnston

Risk is a form of love. We risk nothing for people we don't love, and we risk everything for those we do. The more vulnerable we make ourselves to others, the more opportunity we have for that relationship to grow in trust and mutual appreciation. Since God has enabled us to love one another, He has also called us to take risks for one another. The decision to be a vessel for God's use demands that you take some risks with family, friends, strangers and even enemies.

Duane: The Passerby

My twin brother and I used to live thirty-seven miles apart in rural Indiana. He had a motorcycle I sometimes borrowed to drive from his house to mine. On one such ride, I ran out of gas. All I could do was abandon the motorcycle and begin walking. I walked toward a house about a mile away and knocked on the door, but no one was there. A man drove up, however, and noticed that I was in need.

Many people have been in this situation, but what makes the story worth retelling is what he said when he rolled down the window. This man in his sixties said, "I have never done this before, but God told me to pick you up." I told him I was grateful and hopped in. He not only took me to a gas station, he brought me back to the bike. I was privileged to witness firsthand the transformational moment that this book is about. This man decided that rather than pass me by, he would be used by God to take a risk and help someone in need. We are richer, fuller people when we take these risks. When we refuse to take them, our soul shrinks in a sense. We close ourselves off from others and protect ourselves; and we live a more private life, which, though safer, is also less fulfilling. Apparently, this man had gone sixty years protecting himself and reducing risk, but eventually God extended him an invitation to be used in a new way. This new way was riskier than the ways to which he was accustomed to be sure; nevertheless, it was richer for his soul.

You may likely have an encounter with someone soon that will push your limits of comfort and safety. Someone may ask for one dollar; and as you open your wallet, you may discover you only have a five-dollar bill. Someone may ask to borrow an object that you hold dear. I am not encouraging you to be reckless or careless, but I do encourage you to see that request as a possible invitation from God rather than as a threat or inconvenience. Maybe the right answer is not an automatic "yes," but it might not be an automatic "no" either. Ask God whether He is prompting you to be used to take a risk.

In the parable of the good Samaritan (see Luke 10:25–37), Jesus speaks of this kind of risk. One of the teachers of the law asked Jesus what he must do to inherit eternal life. Jesus answered the question with a story. A Jewish man was robbed and beaten, and his suffering was neglected by a priest and a Levite. What would possess someone to keep on walking instead of stopping to help? We all know the answer, because we have all done it ourselves. Sometimes we fail to get involved because of busyness or even fail to notice because of self-absorption. Sometimes we fear that the cost will be too great as responding may cost our reputation, our time or our money. Some hesitate to respond for fear of liability. In Jesus' story, a hated foreigner eventually came to the aid of the mugging victim. He tended to the man's wounds and paid for his keep at an inn. Jesus said that the Samaritan in this story loved his neighbor as himself and thereby kept the second greatest commandment.

Jim Cymbala, the pastor of the Brooklyn Tabernacle Church, was used by God to take risks among the poor. He recounts many of these risks in *Fresh Wind, Fresh Fire*. On one occasion, he admits being repulsed by the odor of a homeless man he was helping. He sensed God saying to him, "Jim, if you and your wife have any value to me, if you have any purpose in my work—it has to do with this odor."[1] So Jim and his family made a decision to take risks among the poor and needy. In so doing, they made themselves available for God's use.

Jim's actions are consistent with the biblical charge, "Do not forget to entertain strangers, for by so doing some people have entertained angels without knowing it" (Heb. 13:2).

When we see a person in need, we have an opportunity to be used by God. By seeing each act of kindness as potentially for an angel in disguise, we remember that every person represents the image of God. In taking risks to help others, we are faithful to Jesus' commendation that "whatever you did for one of the least of these brothers of mine, you did for me" (Matt. 25:40). We can be used by God to take risks for others.

30

Used to Intercede

*"He saw that there was no man, and wondered that there was no one
to intercede; then his own arm brought him salvation."*

Isaiah 59:16, ESV

The Bible tells us about the importance of a person who chooses to be used as an intercessor. Ezekiel refers to such a person as one who stands in the gap (see 22:30). You can be used in this important way as you stand in the gap on behalf of others. You can be used by God to intercede for others.

Daniel: The Intercessor

The prophet Daniel became a prominent government advisor during the period of the Persian rule in Israel. He advised Kings Nebuchadnezzar, Belshazzar and Ahasuerus. During the reign of these kings, Daniel had visions which revealed that the world would be under constant political turmoil for the next several centuries. Daniel also lived during a time of turmoil for the Jewish people, who had lived in exile after the destruction of the temple and the city of Jerusalem. Daniel knew that he and his people would be living in a foreign country with forbidden food, strange gods and peculiar customs. He understood that this period of captivity and exile would last seventy years, as prophesied by previous prophets. This was a tragic time—not just because the nation was destroyed, but because it became impossible to practice their religion. Their language changed; and it was impossible to celebrate the feasts or festivals commanded in Scripture in the absence of a temple, which was required for sacrifices. For a large part, Judaism was forgotten during this period. This grieved Daniel, so he prayed fervently for his people. Daniel says, "I turned to the Lord God and pleaded with him in prayer and petition, in fasting, and in sackcloth and ashes" (Dan. 9:3).

Daniel was used by God as an intercessor. He knew that his people needed someone to plead their case before God, and he rose to the challenge. These were sacrificial prayers on behalf of others. We read, "At that time I, Daniel, mourned for three weeks. I ate no choice food; no meat or wine touched my lips; and I used no lotions at all until the three weeks were over" (10:2–3). Daniel prayed for his people because they were in exile— captives in the nation of Babylon. After his prayer, God revealed to him that the exile would come to an end soon. What's more, God gave Daniel assurance that after the Jewish people were allowed to return to Jerusalem and rebuild the temple, the Messiah would come and establish his everlasting kingdom.

Pastor Bill Hybels explains the importance of being used by God through prayer.

Prayerless people cut themselves off from God's prevailing power and the frequent result is the familiar feeling of being overwhelmed, overrun, beaten down pushed around, defeated. Surprising numbers of people are willing to settle for lives like that. Don't be one of them. Nobody has to live like that. Prayer is the key to unlocking God's prevailing power in your life.[1]

Hybels notes that God wants to answer our prayers because He loves us, and God is able to answer our prayers because He is the ruler of the universe. Hybels writes, "Take a father's feeling for his children and multiply it exponentially, and you'll know how your heavenly Father feels about you. No one's voice sounds sweeter to God than yours. Nothing in the cosmos would keep him from directing his full attention to your requests."[2]

Think of the people in the Bible who were used by God in prayer.

- Abraham prayed for a son, and God made him the father of many nations (see Gen. 15:1–6).
- Elijah prayed for the life of a widow's son, and he was raised from the dead (see 1 Kings 17:20–22).
- Jonah prayed for deliverance from the fish, and his life was saved (see Jon. 2:1–10).
- A leper prayed for healing, and Jesus healed him (see Matt. 8:2–3).
- Moses prayed for fresh water in the desert, and God provided (see Exod. 15:24–25).
- Solomon prayed for wisdom, and God made him the wisest person in history (see 1 Kings 3:6–14).

- Gideon prayed for proof that God was calling him to deliver the Israelites in battle, and God gave him proof (see Judg. 6:36–40).
- The church prayed for Peter to be released from prison, and he miraculously escaped (see Acts 12:5–10).

The Bible tells us that this power in prayer is available to everyone who calls on the name of the Lord. James explains that you do not have to be a prophet or a Bible hero to be used by God in prayer. He writes, "The prayer of a righteous man is powerful and effective. Elijah was a man just like us. He prayed earnestly that it would not rain, and it did not rain on the land for three and a half years. Again he prayed, and the heavens gave rain, and the earth produced its crops" (James 5:16–18).

31

Used to Submit

"This free-will business is a bit terrifying anyway. It's almost pleasanter to obey and make the most of it."

—Ugo Betti

The Bible clearly teaches that a requirement for being used by God is submitting to authority. Nearly every type of relationship is addressed in Scripture with an admonition to obey and respect those in charge. Because God has instituted these relationships, they are a part of His order. We sabotage our ability to be used by God when we rebel against that design.

Tyler: The Punk

Tyler, a high school student at our church, got into trouble at school nearly every day. He was suspended or given detention regularly for disrespecting authority. Though his attitude was clearly self-defeating and contrary to Scripture, to some extent it made sense to me. I could see what contributed to it. Over several years of working with him, I discovered that he had been abused by nearly every authority figure in his life. As a result, he had developed some sarcastic reactions. One time a teacher told him to sit down. He waved his hands like a magician and said, "Control is an illusion." The teacher was not impressed and gave him a detention. I always thought that instead the teacher should have said, "Then fool me."

Submit to Governing Authorities

Our youth group was returning from a weeklong mission trip to Mexico and had to wait in a three-hour line of vehicles to clear customs and immigration. I normally don't mind the line since I love the fresh churros and tacos you can buy while you wait. On this particular trip, I was towing my camper trailer behind our clearly marked church van. The customs officer was proud of his job and his faith. As I pulled up to his station, he said, "I better look inside the trailer, you know Romans 13:1." The verse says, by the way, "Everyone must submit himself to the governing authorities, for there is no authority except that which God has established. The authorities that exist have been established by God." This verse indicates that as Christians are used by God, He expects us to submit to our government. Usually when I make that point, people object and ask if there are any exceptions. The answer is yes. When Peter was arrested by the Sadducees and warned never to speak in the name of Jesus again, he replied, "We must obey God rather than men!" (Acts 5:29). But unless the governing authorities are asking us to do something that is forbidden in Scripture, Christians should submit to their rulers. Doing so is one way we can be used by God.

Sometimes that submission may be costly and difficult. It may be difficult to see how it pays off. Other times the payoff may be obvious. On another occasion when crossing the customs line—this time after returning from an international flight—my wife and I were traveling with our ten-month-old daughter, Rebekah. My wife was tired and was hoping not to have any "special" treatment on the way back, since she had already been selected for special searches on the previous flight. Then a customs officer spotted us in the crowd and headed straight for us. We thought, *Why among these five hundred passengers did we look the most suspicious?* The officer said to my wife, "Ma'am, please come with me." My normally compliant and unassuming wife, Kristina, said in a defiant huff, "Why?" The officer said, "Never mind. I was going to get you to the front of the line since you look exhausted. But never mind." Obviously, a more submissive tone in this case would have paid off. But we are not asked by God to make that calculation. We are to respond with respectful submission in all cases, except when doing so would violate a command of God. And often, when we act in obedience to God—even against our first inclination—God rewards us with a welcome surprise. On the other hand, when we follow our own will, God often arranges more difficulty. The Bible does not say that we should submit when it is easy or makes sense. The true test of submission is when we sacrifice our desires for the will of another. And it is in this place of sacrifice that we can be used by God.

Submit to Church Leaders

Biblical submission covers many relationships besides citizens to their government. Congregations are also exhorted to submit to their pastors. We read, "Obey your leaders and submit to their authority. They keep watch over you as men who must give an account. Obey them so that their work will be a joy, not a burden, for that would be of no advantage to you" (Heb. 13:17).

During our Friday morning men's Bible study at our church, one of our elders beautifully exercised the concept in this verse. A few of us were commenting on a well-known televangelist. We were not speaking fondly, and we assumed that everyone knew who we were talking about and agreed with the criticism. One of the men in the group named Don must not own a TV, because he didn't know the man who we assumed was a household name. Don figured out, however, that we were speaking about a pastor, and this gracious man sternly warned while shaking his finger, "I don't know who you're talking about, but it sounds like you are disrespecting the Lord's anointed." Then he got even more severe in his reproach and said, "Be careful!" Don was right. We have the liberty to disagree and to expose false teaching, but we do not have liberty to derive pleasure from speaking evil about someone. And our natural inclination should be to submit to our leaders in the church.

Submit to Parents

Children also get confused about their role and purpose as vessels to be used by God. The Bible speaks of the role of submission within the family. Paul writes, "Children, obey your parents in the Lord, for this is right" (Eph. 6:1). Our daughter Natasha came to live with us as a foster child when she was two, but her adoption was not final until she was four years old. After everything was final, we had to change her name at the social security office. Her birth name was Natasha, and we kept it that way, but we just needed to change her last name officially. It was a formality since she could never remember going by any other last name than ours. We were excited about the day, so we made it a special occasion and told her we were going to change her name. She didn't object, and she waited patiently during all the paperwork. After we finished with all the forms, we walked back to the car and started driving home. Then she spoke up as if the anticipation had been killing her and asked, "So, what is it?" All that time she thought she was going to get a new name, not just formalize her name with the government. My wife and I were both endeared and awed by her level of trust and the submission she had to us. She was willing to take on a new name without even knowing what it was going to be! I think of Moses, who proclaimed the fifth commandment, to honor one's father and mother. The commandment came with a promise. Paul paraphrased the promise, "That it may go well with you" (Eph. 6:3). With Natasha's joyful and willing attitude of submission, we could tell that things would indeed go well with her.

Submit to the Word of God

I was teaching a Bible study one night and Vince, one of our college students, asked a question about eating meat. He had come to the conclusion that eating meat was forbidden by God. I was a little concerned since this wasn't our main topic and I didn't want to get too sidetracked. I mentioned 1 Cor. 10:25, which says, "Eat anything sold in the meat market without raising questions of conscience." Then Vince did something extraordinary that I wish I could say has happened more often. He paused as if he had a eureka moment and said, "That changes everything!" Vince is among those who Jesus has blessed. Jesus said, "Blessed . . . are those who hear the word of God and obey it" (Luke 11:28). Vince heard the word of God, and it changed everything. If all of us were as willing to so readily submit to the word of God, we would reap the blessing Jesus promised.

Why We Can Submit Without Going Crazy

The reason we are able to submit to earthly authorities while watching them fail and yet not go crazy is that we know our place in the universe. We know that God is sovereign and we are not. What's more, "We know that in all things God works for the good of those who love him, who have been called according to his purpose" (Rom. 8:28). Confidence in the sovereignty of God is an act of worship and praise. Serenity in the sovereignty of God is a compliment to Him as well. It means that you not only acknowledge that God is in control, but you think He is doing a good job at it. The Bible is clear that as we are used by God, we fit within systems of authority which He has ordained for His purposes. And we can be used with confidence, not in people's ability to exercise authority, but in God's sovereignty.

32

Used to Share Faith

*"How beautiful upon the mountains are the feet of him
who brings good news."*

Isaiah 52:7

One of the most significant ways you will ever be used by God is through the proclamation of the gospel to those who have not yet heard it. You can affect someone else's life for eternity if you make yourself available to be used by God to share the good news of salvation in Christ.

Naaman's Slave Girl: The Evangelist

During the lifetime of the prophet Elisha in Israel (800 BC), there was a high-ranking soldier named Naaman. Naaman was commander of the army of the king of Aram, a nation neighboring Israel. "He was a great man in the sight of his master and highly regarded, because through him the Lord had given victory to Aram. He was a valiant soldier, but he had leprosy. Now bands from Aram had gone out and had taken captive a young girl from Israel, and she served Naaman's wife. She said to her mistress, 'If only my master would see the prophet who is in Samaria! He would cure him of his leprosy'" (2 Kings 5:1–3).

The prophet Elisha had an evangelist in a neighboring nation who sent people to him for healing! This man's slave girl cared enough for her master to encourage him to go see the prophet, and she was confident enough in Elisha's God that she believed the referral would be worthwhile. When Naaman arrived in Samaria, he wasn't sure where Elisha was, so he went to the king of Israel. Ironically, even though the king lived in the same region as Elisha, he was less confident than this distant slave girl. We read that the king tore his clothes when this sick traveler came to him because he could offer no help. Elisha, however, heard about the foreigner and how the king had torn his clothes out of desperation. Elisha asked, "Why have you torn your robes? Have the man come to me and he will know that there is a prophet in Israel" (5:8).

The referral of the slave girl was good. After washing in the Jordan as Elisha instructed, Naaman was healed. And we read of his response, "Then Naaman and all his attendants went back to the man of God. He stood before him and said, 'Now I know that there is no God in all the world except in Israel'" (5:15).

This slave girl, whose name is unknown, was used by God as an evangelist. As a poor young woman living in ignorance in a foreign country, she had heard a report about a prophet of God who could heal, and she believed what she heard. She passed the valuable good news to her master, who saw for himself that the God of Israel is the only true God. This slave girl was used to share her faith. You too can be used by God as a vessel of good news.

Steve Sjogren explains how we can be used by God to share our faith without going crazy.

> The Holy Spirit is the only true evangelist who has ever existed. His is the only power in the universe that can turn a convert into a disciple who looks like Jesus Christ. If the Holy Spirit truly is the only evangelist who has ever been, then we are free to remove the pressure from the wrong places. We can begin seeing ourselves as co-workers with the Holy Spirit, letting him do what only he can do anyway. Our role is to enjoy the flow of God's life through us as we share our joy with others.[1]

It can be intimidating to be used by God as a vessel for the sharing of the good news. Most of the fear in faith sharing, however, results from confusion over our role. If we think our job is to make people change their minds, we will either resign in frustration or persist in frantic frenzy, because we will quickly realize that we cannot determine the response that other people will have.

We can be used by God as vessels for the sharing of the good news. The Bible says, "How beautiful on the mountains are the feet of those who bring good news, who proclaim peace, who bring good tidings, who proclaim salvation, who say to Zion, 'Your God reigns!'" (Isa. 52:7). Your feet can be used by God to bring that beautiful proclamation!

We are surrounded by numerous examples of people "sharing their faith" in a particular person, idea or product. They are filled with zeal and enthusiasm, and they share the news. I called a drywall repairman to fix a hole in a ceiling, and before he left he asked me, "Do you want the acoustic texture removed from the house?" "Oh, do you do that work too?" I asked. "No," he answered, "but a friend of mine asked me years ago if I would ask my clients and refer them to him, so I do that every time." I was struck by his consistent, enthusiastic, selfless discipline to send referrals to his friend's business. In the same way, God can use us as His best referral source!

When my daughter Leah was just four years old, she provided our family an astounding lesson in learning to pay attention to the testimony of an eyewitness. I opened the access panel to our aboveground Jacuzzi in order to fix the heater. When I got the cover off, Leah said, "Daddy, Henry!" Henry was our pet tortoise who we had not seen in over two years. After Henry "ran away," we put up signs in the neighborhood, but we never heard anything, so we figured he buried himself in a hole and maybe died in hibernation. After Leah said, "Daddy, Henry!" I did what many parents feel guilty for doing. I said, "Yeah, uh-huh." In other words, I was too busy working on the repair to pay attention to her. She said "Henry!" again, so I thought she must have seen a water pattern that dripped on the concrete in the shape of a tortoise. She said it a third time; and then I looked where she was pointing and saw Henry, trapped inside the spa equipment.

Since over two years had passed, I was not excited. In fact, I thought I was in for a disgusting, stinky cleanup. I tried to avert her attention and went to get a shovel. Then I thought better, assuming the carcass would fall to pieces when I attempted to pick it up with a shovel, so I decided to move the spa to get everything out. Then Leah said, "He's moving." The first time she spoke, I simply didn't pay attention to her testimony, but this time I gently but firmly disagreed—"No Leah, he died." But Leah insisted, "He's moving." Apparently I learned nothing from the first exchange where I had disregarded her, because I reiterated that she was wrong. She wasn't. Henry had survived over two years without food, and he was just fine. In fact, I researched this afterward and discovered this is no world record.

What our whole family learned is that everyone can be used as a powerful, reliable witness. The testimony of a four-year-old eyewitness trumps logic and predetermined assumptions and paradigms. You too can be used by God as a powerful witness, because your personal experience with God trumps the logic and argument of those who haven't met Him!

33

Used to Forgive

"We read that we ought to forgive our enemies; but we do not read that we ought to forgive our friends."

—Cosimo de Medici

What it means to forgive is often difficult to pinpoint. We know that it does not mean absolving the other person of guilt, and we know forgiving doesn't always require forgetting. It does not mean granting something only God can grant: atonement for sins. Forgiveness does mean, however, having a willingness to preserve the relationship. People who make themselves vessels for God's use become acquainted with forgiveness.

Jenna: The Alcoholic's Daughter

Jenna's father was an alcoholic. She remembers hiding under furniture as a little girl, hoping her parents would stop fighting. She wished the police would take him away on the nights when he came home drunk.

Later, when she was married, as conflict arose, she often responded to conflict with disproportionate fear and anger. At first her husband thought she was just overreacting or that she had a quick temper. Eventually, he realized that she was responding to difficulty in the marriage like a frightened, powerless little girl. Her ability to deal with conflict had not matured with age. They decided that it was time for Jenna to forgive her father. But how do you forgive someone for years of alcoholism, especially if he has not asked for forgiveness? And what if you don't feel like forgiving him? And what if you say you forgive him but nothing changes? Together they went to a lakeside for a picnic. This would be a special memorable day, when Jenna would set an appointment with God and she would forgive her father. She prayed for strength to forgive and healing, and she affirmed the truth that she had forgiven her father. Then she trusted that the feelings of forgiveness would follow.

Forgiveness is like a train—the truth or fact that you have forgiven is the engine, and the feeling of forgiveness that follows is the caboose. The caboose is a real part of the train, but it does not drive it. If you have found it difficult to forgive, do not wait for some overwhelming feeling of forgiveness before you verbally affirm the truth that you are not perfect yourself, and that you forgive the person who sinned against you. You do not need the other person to know you have forgiven him, nor does he have to ask you for forgiveness. This is a private choice separate from what the other person deserves or what you feel. There are probably people in your life who you find the thought of forgiving repulsive. You may have fooled yourself into thinking that you forgave them, but you secretly would be pleased if something bad befell them. God can give you the grace to forgive. The first martyr of the Christian church, Stephen, was stoned to death. And his last words were, "Do not hold this sin against them" (Acts 7:60).

Jesus taught his disciples to have a deep well of forgiveness. He said, "If [your brother] sins against you seven times in a day, and seven times comes back to you and says, 'I repent,' forgive him" (Luke 17:4). We have the ability to extend this kind of undying forgiveness because we are the recipients of undeserved forgiveness from God.

If you have been harboring unforgiveness, it is time to accept the liberating and beautiful challenge from God to grant your enemy what God granted you. Paul wrote, "Therefore, as God's chosen people, holy and dearly loved, clothe yourselves with compassion, kindness, humility, gentleness and patience. Bear with each other and forgive whatever grievances you may have against one another. Forgive as the Lord forgave you" (Col. 3:12–13).

Consider the toll that unforgiveness takes on your soul. It is exhausting and consuming. It's been said that every time you have a thought of unforgiveness, it's like taking a poisonous pill. When we don't forgive, we suffer. We read of the insatiable appetite that unforgiveness creates in Genesis. Jacob stole his brother's birthright and blessing, and Esau hated him for it. We read, "Esau held a grudge against Jacob because of the blessing his father had given him. He said to himself, 'The days of mourning for my father are near; then I will kill my brother Jacob'" (Gen. 27:41). Esau's desire for revenge was understandable, and no one faults him for his anger. But eventually he had a change of heart. After several years of estrangement, the brothers reunited. Jacob was terrified at seeing his angry brother because he did not realize

Esau had forgiven him. We read, "Esau ran to meet Jacob and embraced him; he threw his arms around his neck and kissed him. And they wept" (Gen. 33:4).

An incredible story of forgiveness emerged after the end of slavery in America. Fifty-two black delegates met at Charleston's Zion Church in November 1865 for the Charleston Colored People's Convention. They discussed their response to slavery, and produced the following statement:

> As American chattel slavery has now passed forever away, we would cherish in our hearts no malice nor hatred toward those who were implicated in the crime of slaveholding; but we would extend the right hand of fellowship to all; and would make it our special aim to establish unity, peace, and brotherhood among all men.[1]

David Augsburger explains forgiveness as this: "Forgiving is risking a return to conversation and a resumption of relationship. The two Greek words for forgiveness are translated most clearly as 'to release or set free' and 'to offer a gift of grace.'"[2] In other words, forgiveness means trying again. It means continuing to love. There are people in your life who you need to forgive who don't deserve it. Maybe they haven't asked, and maybe they'll never know you have forgiven them. Yet the Holy Spirit desires to set you free from the bondage of resentment. God wants to use you as a vessel of forgiveness.

34

Used to Forget

"Good, to forgive; Best, to forget! Living, we fret; Dying, we live."
—*Robert Browning in* La Saisiaz

Sometimes, forgiving is not enough; it is even more blessed to forget. Forgetting is a special blessing or ability. We probably can't will ourselves to forget; our only hope is to ask God to be used by Him so much as instruments of His grace that He gives us the blessing of forgetfulness.

Gladys: The Preview Saint

Once our family visited a church where I had served as pastor several years prior. Our family was recognized during the worship service, and as we stood we were thanked for our prior years of service. Those years were difficult at times, and as we were standing my eyes caught glimpses of some of the people who hadn't made things any easier. I glanced at one particular elderly woman named Gladys, and I remembered how on several occasions she had come to me with complaints, bitterness or objections. After the service, we stood in the back and shook hands with the church members as they filed past the exit. Gladys was coming down the line. I wondered what that reunion would be like. I assumed she would shake my hand cordially, but I thought inside that she would be shaking her head disapprovingly.

When she took hold of my hand she said, "Dan, I'm sorry . . ." Here, I thought, was a miracle. A gift just for me. Something I hoped for, wanted, deserved and got! She was going to tell me she was sorry for all she said and did! But she was speaking slowly, and I could tell she was midsentence. She continued, "I'm sorry, but I just can't remember you. My memory is very weak now, and I am told that you were the pastor here, but I just can't remember." My immediate thought was, *How unjust. She should be required to remember everything she said to me. Not only on earth, but even in heaven she should be required to replay those conversations.*

But then I was overcome with pleasure at the goodness of God. This blessed Gladys was fortunate to get a taste of heaven earlier than the rest of us. We have to wait until we're with God to forget all the tears and sorrow, but God blessed her with a preview. None of the things that she said to me years ago will matter in heaven, and they don't matter here on earth. "The grass withers and the flowers fall, but the word of our God stands forever" (Isa. 40:8). Those conversations I had with Gladys will not endure forever. God promises, "I, even I, am he who blots out your transgressions, for my own sake, and remembers your sins no more (43:25).

Even though we have a knack for detailed memory of the way people have sinned against us, God promises the opposite. He says, "For I will forgive their wickedness and will remember their sins no more" (Jer. 31:34).

If God can forget my sins, certainly I can forget the sins of others. That morning, while holding Gladys' hand, I decided that I would be used as an instrument of forgetfulness.

35

Used to Love

"The greatest of these is love."

1 Corinthians 13:3

When the apostle Paul said, "the greatest of these is love," he was speaking of the greatest spiritual gift. Love is, of course, not only the greatest thing God can give us but the greatest thing we can give others. Each person who commits to being used by God has the joy of being a vessel of God's unfailing, unconditional love.

Preston: The Reckless Lover

Driving through the city of Los Angeles on Interstate 110, you can see my friend Preston's home. He and his wife, along with their four children, are missionaries with World Impact. Their mission is to plant churches among the urban poor. I was driving on the freeway with my friend Rick on our way to a downtown restaurant, and I pointed out Preston's house. Rick said that he doesn't get off of the highway in that part of town. He said that he's glad the freeway is elevated and that he always makes certain his car is reliable before he drives through that part of the city. Rick said, "Preston must be stupid to live there, especially with his four kids." For Rick, there is only one possible explanation for why a college-educated man from an affluent family would live in that part of town—stupidity. But Rick knows that Preston is well-educated too and that he's a missionary with World Impact, so he realized that stupid is probably not the best word. He rephrased it—"naïve." He said, "Preston is naïve to think that he can change anything in that part of town, and he is naïve to put his wife and four children in harm's way for the naïve opportunity to try."

"There is," I challenged, "another possibility that drives him to live among his neighbors. It could be that Preston *loves* them, and he *wants* to be used by God as a vessel of love." Maybe it is not Preston's naiveté at all that causes him to live among the poor in the inner city; maybe he is fully aware of the risks and challenges, and is uniquely called and prepared! Jesus exemplified this kind of sacrificial love toward us. He wasn't naïve or stupid when he went to the cross. Instead, He made a conscious decision out of love for us. Jesus said, "Greater love has no one than this, that one lay down his life for his friends" (John 15:13).

Kristina: The Companion

My favorite sport is skiing. My wife is decent at skiing, but she isn't fast. We began skiing together when we were teenagers; and in those young years I learned a lesson that should have been obvious to me, but I learned it the hard way. We would ski down a slope, but since I was faster I would always leave her behind. I became frustrated—not that our skill levels were different, but that it seemed like her values were different. Finally I asked her, "Why did you decide to go skiing?" I felt that if she wasn't going to go fast, what was the point? Her answer was, "to be with you." "Well you're not doing a good job at that," I said. I was getting a sunburn from looking up the mountain all day with my face toward the sun, trying to find her. She was, needless to say, very hurt. She thought it was obvious that the only reason we went skiing together was to spend time with each other, and I thought it was obvious that the only reason anyone goes skiing is to have the constant thrill of speed and danger.

That day I made a decision that would affect the rest of our years together. My time is not to be used simply for my pleasure. My time is to be used as a resource for expressing love to others. Paul encouraged the Corinthians to live with this same attitude. He said, "So whether you eat or drink or whatever you do, do it all for the glory of God" (1 Cor. 10:31). Eat and drink we may, but no activity is to be used for the sake of our own pleasure. In eating, drinking and everything else, we may be used to give glory to God. In glorifying God we obey the two great commandments: to love God and love our neighbor. Jesus commanded us to be used by God as vessels of love. He said, "A new command I give you: Love one another. As I have loved you, so you must love one another" (John 13:34). From Jesus' words, it is obvious that love is not a feeling, nor something foreign that comes over us subconsciously. Instead, love is a conscious decision to act lovingly toward others. But love is also an incredible paradox; the more we act lovingly, the greater our capacity is to love.

We all know we cannot, in our own strength, live up to Jesus' command to love others as He loved us. After all, His manner of loving us was to die for us, while we were in rebellion against Him! Our only hope of being used by God in this way is to let His love fill us and flow through us to others.

36

Used First

*"Greater love has no one than this, that someone
lay down his life for his friends."*

John 15:13, ESV

Many of us are willing to be used by God, but we still
don't want to be used first. We don't want to be
the first to give, the first to apologize, the first to
sacrifice. But by waiting for someone else to go first, we often
begin a painful standoff. I realized this in my marriage and
determined that not only would I be used by God but I am
willing to be used first.

Kristina: The Weaker Vessel?

After my wife and I had been married for ten years, we
didn't get in arguments very often, but I still had not matured as a husband to the point where we could argue pro-
ductively and with self-control. During one particular argument, I thought I would try an experiment. Experiments

in relationships are dangerous; I don't recommend them. That's because, like less reputable scientists, we often set out to prove our hypothesis, and we taint the circumstances to ensure that our prediction is validated. So over a decade I had been collecting data in my mind of every argument my wife and I had ever had, and I had been keeping track of what percent of the time I had taken the initiative to reconcile versus what percent of the time she took the initiative. Admittedly, my memory could be a little cloudy; but according to my data, I was the person to say that I was sorry first 100 percent of the time.

So the experiment I had in mind was to see what would happen if I refused to be the first to apologize or to try to move the argument in a more positive direction. It didn't go well. I want you to know that as a vessel capable of being used by God or by Satan, I left my precious wife crawled up in a ball on our bed crying. That is the evil of which I am capable. Then my wife delivered what I thought was a pretty low blow. She quoted the Bible. Specifically, she referenced 1 Peter 3.7. She said, "Can't you see I'm the weaker vessel?" I retorted, "Well, that's obvious." My tone of voice didn't indicate that I thought she had employed a pertinent use of Scripture; instead, I implied, "I don't like what I see." Inwardly I knew she was right, so I confessed and repented of my sin against her and against God.

I learned a life-changing lesson that day, and I was confronted with a decision about how I would be used. Would I be used first? In other words, would I allow God to use me first for reconciliation? Or would I require God to use me second?

My wife was absolutely right that Peter wrote, "Husbands, in the same way be considerate as you live with your wives, and treat them with respect as the weaker partner and as heirs with you of the gracious gift of life, so that nothing will hinder your prayers" (1 Pet. 3:7). It is undeniable that the Bible endows husbands with great responsibility, and that at the creation of the world, God endowed husbands with great strength to be able to show self-control and be used first.

Now I am not saying that wives should make a decision to be the second to apologize. No one should make that decision. In fact, every person should resolve that he or she will be used by God to be the first to reconcile. In fact, even though Paul writes in Ephesians that wives should submit to their husbands, he says that, nevertheless, the concept of mutual submission applies to every Christian. The apostle wrote, "Submit to one another out of reverence for Christ" (Eph. 5:21).

But after writing that all Christians should submit to one another, Paul does say that husbands have and are equipped for a unique burden. Many Christians have probably heard and wrestled with the exhortation for wives to submit to their husbands (5:22). The verse is controversial and has sparked plenty of debates. But when I read the passage, I ask myself, "Who got the short end of the stick?" Sure, wives are encouraged to submit to their husbands, and that can be difficult in even the best of marriages. But what are the husbands commanded to do? "Love your wives, just as Christ loved the church" (5:25). True, that does sound much easier than submitting. It does sound like the wives got the apple on the bottom of the barrel. But how did Christ love the church? "And gave himself up for her" (5:25). That's not only a tall order; it's practical annihilation.

If husbands are to love their wives in the same way that Christ loved the church, which was a total self-sacrificing love, then they will make themselves available to God to be used first to love and will take the initiative to reconcile or apologize. But what about the wife whose husband just simply isn't going to go first? Or what about other relationships outside of marriage? What about the child whose parents are clearly not going to go first? While I have expressed the biblical exhortation for husbands, the concept applies to everyone. If we are all to submit ourselves to one another, then in all relationships we should make ourselves available to be used by God first. Jesus exemplified this truth in His own life, and demanded the same of His followers. He said, "If anyone wants to be first, he must be the very last, and the servant of all" (Mark 9:35).

37

Used for Grace

"But for the grace of God, there goes John Branford."
—John Branford

Whether or not Christians should aim for perfection themselves has been debated much since the Reformation. Some argue that perfection is possible because, after all, the Bible says twice, "Be holy, because I am holy" (1 Pet. 1:16). They reason that God would not have given us a command that we cannot keep. And not to aim for perfection seems self-defeating. Who, after all, is making us sin? If no one is compelling us to sin, then surely we can go the next hour without sinning. And if we can go the next hour, we can go the rest of the day (and so on). We take ourselves off the hook if we say we cannot be perfect. Others argue, however, that God did indeed give us a command that we cannot keep. He gave us this command to "be perfect" precisely to show us that we cannot keep all God's commands. We will never be saved by our own effort, so God demonstrated how dependent we are upon His grace by giving us commands that we cannot keep. This view also has biblical support, as Paul said, "Therefore the Law has become our tutor to *lead us* to Christ, so that we may be justified by faith" (Gal. 3:24, NASB).

Dylan: The Perfectionist

A father recently told me that his son Dylan pinkie promises every morning (that's when you shake pinkie fingers to seal the promise) that he will be good that day. He was pleased with his child's effort and hoped his son would live up to the promise. I was concerned, however, when I heard about this daily deal, because the day's goal seems to be misguided. I do not hope that the people around me will be perfect. Instead, I hope that when they sin against me, we will find resolution. Dylan is probably hoping for the right thing by trying to be perfect. But Dylan's father is not hoping for the right thing for two reasons: first, it will not happen, and second, Dylan's perfection is out of his control. As a vessel for God's use, Dylan's father should instead be hoping that when his child sins, he responds the way God does to us.

I am certain that regardless of whether we should aim for perfection ourselves or not, we should not have this expectation of others. From birth my mother told me, "Danny, you worry about Danny and your brother Kenny will worry about Kenny." It is not our place to put the expectation of perfection on others, even if we aim for it ourselves. In addition, we know that the people around us will continue to sin. This is not a condemnation or judgment. On the contrary, it is a merciful realization. We must expect that people will continue to act in accordance with their nature and their will. To do otherwise is cruel. No mother bird expects her fledgling to fly, and no swim coach expects his trainee to hold her breath for ten minutes. It is merciful to expect from others only what is truly possible.

Author Tedd Tripp explains why the expectation that people you love will continue to be sinful is merciful.

> Young Albert was a deceitful child. He sneaked around behind his father's back. He lied even when it was not advantageous. Often he would steal money from his parents. His father insisted on interpreting his behavior as immaturity. Albert was immature, but that was not the reason he was untrustworthy. The reason he could not be trusted is that he was a sinner. Albert's dad was unable to help his son until he began to see that Al's behavior reflected a heart that had defected from God.[1]

When children lie, many parents are tempted to say, "Why did you lie to me?" I fight the urge to ask that question. The reason I refuse to ask it is that I know the answer and they don't. They lie to me because they act in accordance with their nature. They and I are born sinners. It is our nature to lie. This nature must be changed if we are to have any hope. Such a change only occurs when we are born again. Rather than ask why they lied to me, I tell them why they lied: "You lied because we are all born with a sinful nature. It is a sin to lie. For your sake, the sake of our family and the glory of God, you must repent of your lie."

Recognizing that it is our original nature to sin is liberating because it helps us make sense of the world and the people around us. It is merciful because it gives us realistic expectations of the people around us. We expect them to sin because we know that they are wretches like us who were saved by amazing grace.

Extending this grace to others is the natural and necessary result of recognizing that we are all bound to sin. But the Bible tells us to be careful whenever we show mercy to others. There is always a cost or trade-off. Jude writes, "Snatch others from the fire and save them; to others show mercy, mixed with fear—hating even the clothing stained by corrupted flesh" (23). Every time we show mercy, we do so at a cost. To continue being merciful to someone implicitly sends the message that his behavior will continue to be tolerated. So every time we show mercy, we should have a little fear that the other person will continue to sin. We should not ask, therefore, how many times we should show mercy but how many times God is calling us to be His vessel of grace.

When is showing mercy the best thing for the other person? If your husband lied to you, ask God whether showing mercy to him is the best thing for his discipleship. If your daughter cheated on a test, ask God if showing mercy is the best thing for her growth. You may be used by God as an instrument to demonstrate His unfailing mercy for us. We know that grace and mercy are in His character, for seven times the Bible reminds us that "the LORD is compassionate and gracious, slow to anger, abounding in love" (Ps. 103:8).

Ask God whether showing mercy is the best thing for the other person's growth. If so, encourage that person. I call this "grace through strength." Sometimes we show mercy to someone out of weakness. We are terrified to confront the other person, we are exhausted or we think it will be pointless. Failing to confront at these times is not really mercy; it is cowardice. But when we make the conscious choice to show grace to someone because it is best for them, we are in a place of great strength. My point here is that it has to be okay that things are not perfect. No marriage is perfect. No workplace is perfect. No children are perfect. No friendship is perfect. If we keep searching for perfection, we will continue wandering and will become frustrated and cruel.

The ultimate goal of relationships, therefore, should be resolution rather than perfection. When someone sins against us, our goal should be to identify the sin, share our grief, ask for an apology and, Lord willing, receive repentance from the other person. The more this process repeats itself, the more we become accustomed to grace. And the more we see grace acted out, the more we become vessels for God's use.

38

Gifted for Use

"Now concerning spiritual gifts, brothers,
I do not want you to be uninformed."

1 Corinthians 12:1, ESV

One of the clearest teachings in Scripture about our usability to God is the concept of spiritual gifts. We read, "There are different kinds of gifts, but the same Spirit. There are different kinds of service, but the same Lord. There are different kinds of working, but the same God works all of them in all men" (1 Cor. 12:4–6).

From piecing together the several passages about spiritual gifts, we come up with what is still undoubtedly a partial list of the ways God has "worked in all people" a unique way to contribute to the world and the church:

- Teaching
- Administration
- Leadership

- Preaching
- Knowledge
- Mercy
- Evangelism
- Helps
- Giving
- Hospitality
- Prophecy
- Healing
- Encouragement
- Faith
- Service
- Wisdom
- Speaking in tongues
- Interpretation of tongues
- Miracles

God has distributed the array of gifts within the church in His wisdom so that He can use His people. These gifts are fit for the needs of the body of Christ. Paul elaborates on their purpose:

> It was [God] who gave some to be apostles, some to be prophets, some to be evangelists, and some to be pastors and teachers, to prepare God's people for works of service, so that the body of Christ may be built up until we all reach unity in the faith and in the knowledge of the Son of God and become mature, attaining to the whole measure of the fullness of Christ. (Eph. 4:11–13)

Every person in the church is indispensable to the kingdom of God. Rick Warren explains, "God gives us different passions so that everything he wants done in the world will get done."[1] That means God has gifted you in a unique way to be used by Him.

Authors Henry and Mel Blackaby explain the role and purpose of spiritual gifts in the church:

> Spiritual gifts are bestowed on believers according to the purposes of God and distributed by the sovereign wisdom of God. Our spiritual gifts never belong to us: they're an expression of the Holy Spirit doing the Father's will.[2]

Perhaps you don't know what your gift is, or you doubt whether you even have anything to contribute. Mel and Henry Blackaby encourage us with these words:

> We hear people complaining about the talents and skills they lack, then concluding, "I don't have anything to offer God." That's likely true, but what does that have to do with the Holy Spirit working in your life? When He's present, it doesn't matter what you can or cannot do. If you don't have a lot of natural talent, you can thank God that you're the perfect vessel for him to show Himself powerful to you. In your weakness, He is strong. You are the person in whom he can do his best work, for he will get all the glory.[3]

I often hear people tell me that they are not getting much out of church. They know that churches are infamous for potlucks, and they seem to have applied the potluck thinking to the whole rest of their church experience. They came, they didn't see anything they liked and now they are going to leave. But if the church is like a potluck, who shows up empty-handed? Children, mostly, and maybe a few young adults who haven't figured out that they aren't children anymore. So when people tell me they aren't getting anything out of church, I ask them what they brought. When you are a vessel for God's use, He expects you to show up at church with something. God says, "No one is to appear before me empty-handed" (Exod. 23:15). Mel and Henry Blackaby realize that many people just aren't sure what they are supposed to bring.

> Do you sense that God wants to use your life, but you thought you had nothing to offer him? Don't merely look at what you have to offer the world; seek the heart of God and allow his spirit to work through you. He'll touch the world in ways you could never touch it on your own. Perhaps the Holy Spirit has just invited you to a greater task in the work of God's kingdom.[4]

There are numerous books and online surveys to help you discover your spiritual gifts and find your unique niche in the kingdom of God. Invest the time, prayer and study to unleash God's potential for you. You were gifted for God's use.

39

Used for Eternity

"Whatever may happen to you was prepared for you from all eternity; and the implication of causes was from eternity spinning the thread of your being."

—Marcus Aurelius

Have you ever wondered what we'll do in heaven? Will we be disembodied spirits who float around feeling good and happy? Some people imagine that they will be doing whatever they enjoyed the most on earth, but they must admit such a concept of heaven is quite self-centered and doesn't really fit with the concept of the church as a body or community. In Scripture we get an answer to this question. The apostle John was caught up to heaven and got a glimpse, so he should know. His time in heaven revealed some of the activities that go on there. He says of the twenty-four elders who are seated before God's throne, "Day and night they never stop saying: 'Holy, holy, holy is the Lord God Almighty, who was, and is, and is to come'" (Rev. 4:8). That's what the elders are doing before God's throne. Does it sound exhausting or boring? Is there some sense of relief knowing that those who never stop singing God's praises are the twenty-four elders but not necessarily all those in heaven? John also tells us what the great multitude does in heaven:

> After this I looked and there before me was a great multitude that no one could count, from every nation, tribe, people and language, standing before the throne and in front of the Lamb. They were wearing white robes and were holding palm branches in their hands. And they cried out in a loud voice: "Salvation belongs to our God, who sits on the throne, and to the Lamb." All the angels were standing around the throne and around the elders and the four living creatures. They fell down on their faces before the throne and worshiped God, saying: "Amen! Praise and glory and wisdom and thanks and honor and power and strength be to our God for ever and ever. Amen!" (7:9–12)

You: The Worshiper

Some people admit to a bit of a letdown when they find out that worship is what happens in heaven. It strikes them as monotonous. The Bible never says that this is the only activity in heaven, but it does say it is the activity of highest importance related in Scripture.

If you're worried about heaven sounding boring, there are other things mentioned in the Bible. Jesus said He went to prepare a room and a great wedding feast for us, and we will participate in the marriage of the Groom (Christ) with the bride (the church). Jesus told us to store up for ourselves treasures in heaven, and the Bible teaches that there are varying rewards for believers based on what they do here on earth. Ezekiel describes the city, landscape and buildings, including the temple, in heaven. So there are other things going on. But the mention of these other things in heaven is not meant to assure us that we won't get bored or that there will be enough things to occupy us and keep us happy. If there are other activities, they take a backseat to center stage where the important story unfolds. John describes what he sees at the center of it all:

> Then I saw a Lamb, looking as if it had been slain, standing in the center of the throne, encircled by the four living creatures and the elders. He had seven horns and seven eyes, which are the seven spirits of God sent out into all the earth. He came and took the scroll from the right hand of him who sat on the throne. And when he had taken it, the four living creatures and the twenty-four elders fell down before the Lamb. Each one had a harp and they were holding golden bowls full of incense, which are the prayers of the saints. And they sang a new song: "You are worthy to take the scroll and to open its seals, because you were slain, and with your blood you purchased men for God from every tribe and language and people and nation. You have made them to be a kingdom and priests to serve our God, and they will reign on the earth." (Rev. 5:6–10)

In this song that the elders sing, we see that the great multitude in heaven has been prepared to serve God as priests. This is what you were made for and how you will spend eternity. You were created, preserved, called and tended by God so you can be used by Him as a vessel of praise.

PART FIVE

How to Be Used by God

40

Steps to Being Used

This book has recounted the stories of people who were used by others, used by the devil and used by God. You are no exception. You have your own stories of how you have been used in each of these ways. There are also a variety of ways that you can be used by God once you make yourself available to Him. As a conclusion, I offer four steps for you to be used by God.

1. Recognize how you have been used by others. It will be liberating to recognize that you have been used by others because this awareness protects you from falling into the same trap again. Recognize that the devil has played you against the most important people in your life and that other people have used you for their own gain or pleasure. (Admittedly, you have used others for selfish purposes as well.)

2. Determine to be used by God. The people who were used by God in this book made a conscious decision. They purposefully chose to be used by God. Now comes a time of decision for you. Will you be enthused by the Holy Spirit? Have you been transfused by new life in Christ? Will you accept your new identity as one excused from sin? Look at the list of ways people are used by God in chapter 38, and determine that you will be available in the same ways. Decide that your life will be reused with new purpose.

3. Define the purpose of your relationships. Each of your relationships serves a purpose related to your design as a vessel for God's use. For example, as a married person, your purpose is to be used as an instrument in discipling your spouse. The purpose of that relationship is to know each other and achieve true intimacy and connection. The goal is to reflect the image of God to each other, which is done in the union where two become one. As a parent, your purpose is to be used by God to disciple your children. God is using you as an example of the way He works with each of us. Each relationship has a purpose. Define how you will be used by God in your relationships.

4. Pray to be used. Look at the prayer of Saint Francis in chapter 2 and make it your own. Pray that God will guard you from being used by others. Pray that God will help you identify when you are being used by the Enemy. And pray that in all relationships and in all situations, you will be used by God.

Jurgis: The Epiphany

Upton Sinclair's classic *The Jungle* aptly illustrates how transformative the moment can be when a man realizes who he has been used by and what he can be used for. Jurgis, the hero of the story, was a Lithuanian immigrant who began working in the stockyards of Chicago around 1900. His welcome to America entailed a series of events, over several years, that made it clear to him that life in the New World is about being used by others for their selfish gain. He was duped by a realtor into buying a ramshackle home that was purportedly new. In the same transaction, he was duped by the bank into a trap that allowed the bank to capture the whole life savings of a dozen immigrants and led to the eventual repossession of the home. And the stockyard company Jurgis worked for tried to squeeze every last drop of profit out of the animals they butchered and the immigrants they essentially enslaved.

The reader desperately hopes that Jurgis will retain his innocence and prevent himself from becoming jaded. But eventually, Jurgis accepts the use of other human beings for one's own gain as the only way of life for survivors. Though initially repulsive to him, the thought of using others becomes his specialty. He begins working for organized crime, registering immigrants in the political parties and paying those new voters to elect corrupt officials. And as long as Jurgis works for those criminals and corrupt politicians, he is fed, clothed, kept out of jail and paid.

That changes when a strike breaks out and Jurgis finds himself out of work and no longer useful to the politicians or criminals. He becomes a hungry, shivering, vagabond. The turning point is poignant and powerful. Jurgis stumbles into a political rally and listens to the speaker. It is at this point that he realizes that all his life he has been used by others—when times were bad, and even when they were good. He determines to no longer let others set the agenda. From now on, he declares, he will decide how he is used.

> The audience came to its feet with a yell; men waved their arms, laughing aloud in their excitement. And Jurgis was with them, he was shouting to tear his throat; shouting because he could not help it, because the stress of his feeling was more than he could bear. There was an unfolding of vistas before him, a breaking of the ground beneath him, an upheaving, a stirring, a trembling; he felt himself suddenly a mere man no longer—there were powers within him undreamed of, there were demon forces contending, age long wonders struggling to be born; and he sat oppressed with pain and joy, while a tingling stole down into his fingertips, and his breath came hard and fast. All that he had ever felt in his whole life seemed to come back to him at once, and with one new emotion, hardly to be described . . . There was a falling in of all the pillars of his soul, the sky seemed to split above him—he stood there, with his clenched hands upraised, his eyes bloodshot, and the veins standing out purple in his face, roaring in the voice of a wild beast, frantic, incoherent, maniacal. And when he could shout no more he still stood there, gasping, and whispering hoarsely to himself: "By God! By God! By God!"[1]

After the speech, the world made sense to Jurgis. It became clear to him that the timeless characteristic of human interaction was for people to use one another. He was used by banks, used by employers, used by criminals and used by politicians. Likewise, he had used others for his own gain. But after the speech, Jurgis determined that his future life would have purpose. Rather than be used as a pawn or victim to further the selfish schemes of others, Jurgis would be used as a selfless vessel for the benefit of others.

Have you had a similar "aha" moment? Have you had a defining moment when you realized that you have been used by others? Have you seen how you have been used by the devil? Even more importantly, have you considered how you will be used by God? Pray that in every relationship and in every situation you will ask, "God, how will You use me?"

Used by God: The "Normal" Christian Life

When we were ten years old, my identical twin brother and I were interested in seeing what church was about. Our parents had never taken us to church before. At the time, neither of them believed in God; but we had some friends who went to church, and we were intrigued. Some combination of curiosity, the providence of God and unanswered existential questions such as, "Why are we here?" led to our gumption to ask our parents, "Can we go to church?"

Our parents were supportive of whatever we pursued, but they did have two strong criteria. They said we could go to church wherever we wanted, but it couldn't be Jehovah's Witness or a Catholic church. Their rationale was interesting. My mother had some family members who were Jehovah's Witness, and she thought the religion was weird. She had seen how the members of the Kingdom Hall shunned those who walked away, and this was hurtful to my mom. But the rationale for why we could not be Catholic has haunted me ever since. My mom and dad both agreed that we could not be Catholic because it "would require too much of a life change." Consider that haunting indictment on the Protestant church! What was my parent's impression of the

Protestant church? No life change necessary. They figured that as long as we went to a Protestant church, our family's identity and routine were safe.

My twin brother became a missionary, I became a pastor and our parents saw that their assumption of safety was wrong. But who could blame them for making the assumption that no life change would be necessary when all too often that is what the world sees in Christians—no great difference.

I hope you will open yourself up to being a vessel for God's use. Identify how you have been used by the devil and how other people have used you, and determine that from this day forward, you will be used by God, no matter the cost.

Soon the devil will tempt you with a sin that keeps haunting you; then is your chance to say, "I will not be used by the devil in his plan to steal, kill and destroy." Or someone more familiar, and perhaps even well-intentioned, will try to use you for their own purposes. Quickly identify that you are about to be used by others and determine, "I'll be used by God instead."

The next time your spouse makes you angry, ask "God, how can I be used as an instrument of Your instruction in this case?" When your child disobeys, pray, "God, how would You use me as a tool of discipleship at this time?" When your coworker talks behind your back, say to yourself, "I am used as an instrument of God's grace, forgiveness and forgetfulness." When you see the beggar on the freeway off-ramp, determine, "I will be used by God as an instrument of comfort." When you see an intolerable situation in public, seek whether God would use you to confront it.

In the past, you have been overused, confused and abused. But now you are enthused by the Holy Spirit, transfused with new life and excused from your sin. You are neither used up nor useless. You are not simply useful, as you are not just an object; you are ready to be reused in a new way by God. Everything changes when you approach life with the determination to be used by God. So the question is, *Who's Using You?*

Notes

Chapter 1: Ways We Are Used

1. Neil T. Anderson, *The Bondage Breaker: Overcoming Negative Thoughts, Irrational Feelings, Habitual Sins* (Eugene: Harvest House Publishers, 1993), 42.
2. For a summary of these theories, see Wayne Grudem, *Systematic Theology: An Introduction to Biblical Doctrine* (Leicester, England: Inter-Varsity Press, 1994), 549–552.

Chapter 2: A Prayer to Be Used

1. Rick Warren, *The Purpose Driven Life: What on Earth Am I Here For?* (Grand Rapids: Zondervan, 2002), 19.
2. Ibid., 20.
3. Ibid., 53.
4. Ibid., 54.

Chapter 4: Used Up

1. Joni Eareckson and Steve Estes, *A Step Further* (New York: Bantam Books, 1978), xi.
2. Ibid., 16.
3. Ibid., 27.

Chapter 5: Use(ful)

1. Henry T. Blackaby and Claude V. King, *Experiencing God: Knowing and Doing the Will of God* (Nashville: Lifeway Press, 1990), 28–29.

Chapter 6: (Ab)used

1. C.S. Lewis, "Letter IX," in *The Screwtape Letters* (New York: Macmillan, 1944), 112.

Chapter 7: Used to Enable

1. Henry Cloud and John Townsend, *Boundaries: When to Say Yes, How to Say No to Take Control of Your Life* (Grand Rapids: Zondervan, 1992), 33.
2. Ibid., 38.
3. Ibid., 103.

Chapter 9: Used Emotionally

1. James Dobson, *Love Must Be Tough: New Hope for Marriages in Crisis* (Carol Stream: Tyndale, 1996), 26.
2. Ibid., 27.

Chapter 11: (Conf)used

1. *Westminister Shorter Catechism* 1646, http://www.westminsterconfession.org/confessional-standards/the-westminster-shorter-catechism.php
2. John Piper, *Let the Nations Be Glad!: The Supremacy of God in Missions* (Grand Rapids: Baker Books, 1993), 51.

Chapter 14: Used to Tempt

1. Michael White, *Maps of Narrative Practice* (New York: W. W. Norton and Company Inc., 2007), 24–25.

Chapter 15: Used to Promote Legalism

1. Charles Swindoll, *The Grace Awakening: Believing in Grace Is One Thing. Living It Is Another* (Nashville: Word Publishing, 1996), 78.

Chapter 16: (Enth)used

1. Billy Graham, *The Holy Spirit: Activating God's Power in Your Life* (Waco: Word Books, 1978), 122.

Chapter 17: (Transf)used

1. John Piper, *Don't Waste Your Life* (Wheaton: Crossway, 2007), 12.
2. Ibid., 17.
3. Ibid., 28.
4. Ibid., 29.
5. Ibid., 33.
6. Ibid., 37.
7. Ibid., 33.
8. Ibid., 36.

Chapter 18: (Exc)used

1. Victor Hugo, "Chapter 12: The Bishop Works," Vol. 1, book 2 in *Les Miserables* (France, 1862).

Chapter 19: (Re)used

1. Fyodor Dostoyevsky, *Crime and Punishment*, Google Books, 500.

Chapter 20: Used in Parenting

1. Tedd Tripp, *Shepherding a Child's Heart* (Wapwallopen, PA: Shepherds Press, 1995), 32.
2. Ibid., 28.
3. Ibid., 30.

Chapter 21: Used in Marriage

1. Larry Crabb, *The Marriage Builder: A Blueprint for Couples and Counselors* (Grand Rapids: Zondervan, 1992), 19.
2. Ibid., 39.
3. Ibid., 52.
4. Ibid., 54.
5. Ibid., 55.

Chapter 24: Used to Confront

1. David Augsburger, *Caring Enough to Confront: How to Understand and Express Your Deepest Feelings Toward Others* (Ventura: Regal Books, 1981), 10.

Chapter 27: Used to Comfort

1. Herman Melville, *Moby Dick* (New York, 1851), 62.

Chapter 28: Used to Encourage

1. John Trent and Gary Smalley, *The Blessing* (Nashville: Thomas Nelson, 2004), 12.
2. Ibid., 18.
3. Ibid., 19.

Chapter 29: Used to Take Risks

1. Jim Cymbala, *Fresh Wind, Fresh Fire: What Happens When God's Spirit Invades the Hearts of His People* (Grand Rapids: Zondervan, 1997), 142.

Chapter 30: Used to Intercede

1. Bill Hybels, *Too Busy Not to Pray: Slowing Down to Be with God* (Downers Grove: Inter-Varsity Press, 1998), 16.
2. Ibid., 28.

Chapter 32: Used to Share Faith

1. Steve Sjogren, *Conspiracy of Kindness: A Unique Approach to Sharing the Love of Jesus* (Ventura: Regal Books, 2003), 50.

Chapter 33: Used to Forgive

1. Donald W. Shriver, *An Ethic for Enemies: Forgivness in Politics*(New York: Oxford University Press, 1995), 176.
2. David Augsburger, *The New Publishers Freedom of Forgiveness* (Chicago: Moody, 2000), 29.

Chapter 37: Used for Grace

1. Tedd Tripp, *Shepherding a Child's Heart,* 23.

Chapter 38: Gifted for Use

1. Rick Warren, *The Purpose Driven Life,* 293.
2. Henry Blackaby and Mel Blackaby, *What's So Spiritual About Your Gifts?* (Colorado Springs: Multnomah Books, 2004), 19.
3. Ibid., 21.
4. Ibid., 46.

Chapter 40: Steps to Being Used

1. Upton Sinclair, "Chapter 28," in *The Jungle* (1906), 285-286.

PUBLICATIONS

Fort Washington, PA 19034

This book is published by CLC Publications, an outreach of CLC Ministries International. The purpose of CLC is to make evangelical Christian literature available to all nations so that people may come to faith and maturity in the Lord Jesus Christ. We hope this book has been life changing and has enriched your walk with God through the work of the Holy Spirit. If you would like to know more about CLC, we invite you to visit our website:

www.clcusa.org

To know more about the remarkable story of the founding of CLC International we encourage you to read

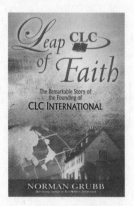

LEAP OF FAITH

Norman Grubb

Paperback
Size 5¹/₄ x 8, Pages 248
ISBN: 978-0-87508-650-7
ISBN (*e-book*): 978-1-61958-055-8

"Larry Smith has written a work that has been actually utilized and shaped in the crucible of real ministry, not in the ivory tower of theory."
—Dr. Eric Mason, author of *Manhood Restored*

J·E·S·U·S LIFE

CONNECTED LIVING IN A DISCONNECTED WORLD

LARRY SMITH

JESUS LIFE

Larry Smith

Jesus Life offers a simple yet compelling strategy to help believers connect to Jesus. Overwhelmed by the hustle and bustle of life, believers are often distracted and need guidance to move in a direction that makes Jesus, not only theoretically but also practically, the focus of their lives.

Paperback
Size 5^1/$_4$ x 8, Pages 251
ISBN: 978-1-61958-201-9
ISBN (*e-book*): 978-1-61958-202-6

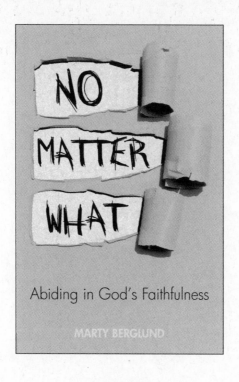

NO MATTER WHAT

Marty Berglund

As stress, temptation, and hardship tug and tear at reality, it is often difficult to see that God has a plan for our lives. *No Matter What* reminds us that God is in control and that we can abide safely in His faithfulness - despite our past and present circumstances. Using the Genesis narrative of Joseph as a backdrop, Marty Berglund challenges readers to live victoriously through God's steadfastness and love.

Paperback
Size 5¹/₄ x 8, Pages 158
ISBN: 978-1-61958-199-9
ISBN (*e-book*): 978-1-61958-200-2

LIFE AS WORSHIP

John Kitchen

Life as Worship explores the life and psalms of Asaph to understand what it means to live a life of worship. This study of Asaph's writings gives readers insight into the psalms' various applications to all seasons of life, including: thankfulness, mourning, reflection, faithfulness and revival.

Paperback
Size 5^1/$_4$ x 8, Pages 267
ISBN: 978-1-61958-162-3
ISBN (*e-book*): 978-1-61958-163-0

Foreword by Collin Hansen

RONNIE MARTIN

STOP YOUR COMPLAINING

FROM GRUMBLING TO GRATITUDE

STOP YOUR COMPLAINING

Ronnie Martin

Stop Your Complaining explores the often-overlooked sin of grumbling and explains how Christians can adopt an attitude of gratitude and humility. Through stories of men and women of the Bible, cultural figures and even the author himself, *Stop Your Complaining* explores the relationship between discontent and gratefulness.

Paperback
Size 5¹/₄ x 8, Pages 144
ISBN: 978-1-61958-205-7
ISBN (*e-book*): 978-1-61958-206-4